The Fatal Bullet

NBM Comics

BIBLIOGRAPHY

The facts contained in *The Fatal Bullet* conform to the following sources:

Balch, William Ralston, *The Life of James Abram Garfield*. (Philadelphia, J.C. McCurdy & Co., 1881

Boller, Paul F., *Presidential Anecdotes*. (New York, Oxford University Press, 1981)
    Presidential Campaigns. (New York, Oxford University Press, 1984)
    Presidential Wives. (New York, Oxford University Press, 1988)

Conwell, Russell, *The Life, Speeches and Public Services of James A. Garfield*. (Boston, B.B. Russell, 1881)

Donovan, Robert J., *The Assassins*. (New York, Popular Library, 1962)

Kelly, Tom, *Murders: Washington's Most Famous Murder Stories*. (Washington DC, Washingtonian Books, 1976)

Maury, William M., *Washington DC Past & Present*. (New York, CBS Publications, 1975)

Panati, Charles, *Panati's Extraordinary Endings of Practically Everything and Everybody*. (New York, Harper & Row, 1989)

✶ Peskin, Allan, *Garfield*. (Kent State University, 1978)

Robertson, Archie, "Murder Most Foul." (American Heritage, Vol. XV, No. 5, August, 1964)

NBM
185 Madison Ave. Ste. 1504
New York, N.Y. 10016
http://www.nbmpub.com

ISBN 1-56163-228-7
Library of Congress Catalog Card Number 99-70727
©1999 Rick Geary

5   4   3   2   1

Comicslit is an imprint and
trademark of

NANTIER · BEALL · MINOUSTCHINE
Publishing inc.
new york

THE FATAL BULLET.

PRESIDENT
JAMES A. GARFIELD
THE ASSASSIN
CHAS. J. GUITEAU

A TRUE ACCOUNT OF THE

ASSASSINATION,

Lingering Pain, Death, and Burial of

JAMES A. GARFIELD,

TWENTIETH PRESIDENT of the United States.

ALSO INCLUDING

The Inglorious Life and Career of THE DESPISED ASSASSIN

GUITEAU.

ADAPTED & ILLUSTRATED BY

RICK GEARY

THE TWO ROADS

WHICH EVERY BOY, AS HE JOURNEYS TO MANHOOD, MAY TRAVEL, THE RESULT OF SURROUNDING CIRCUMSTANCES, FAVORABLE OR OTHERWISE.

"HAPPY, PROSPEROUS LIFE."	"DOWNWARD PATH"
PRESIDENT	THE ASSASSIN
JAMES A. GARFIELD	**CHARLES J. GUITEAU**

A FRONTIER BOYHOOD OF HARD WORK AND PIETY.

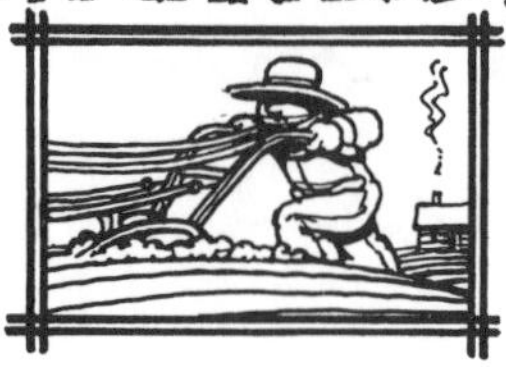

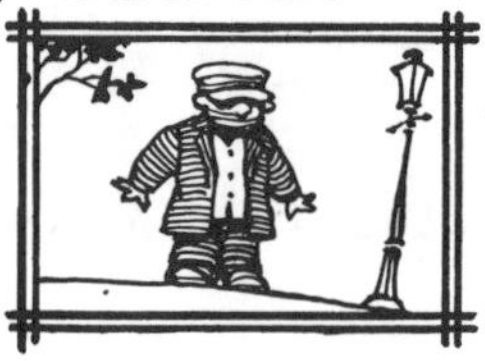

A CHILDHOOD LOST AND LOVE-LESS.

A YOUTH IMMERSED IN STUDY AND SCHOLARSHIP.

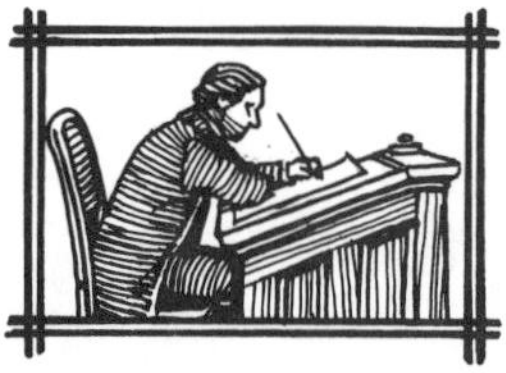

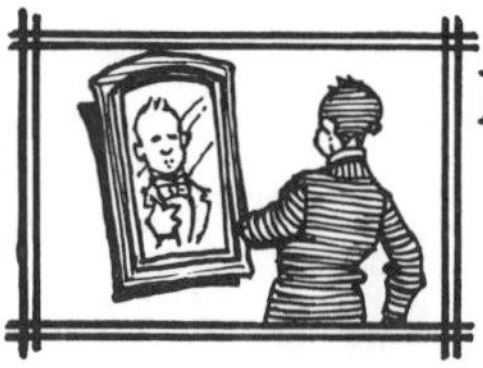

EARLY YEARS WASTED UPON DAY-DREAMING AND FRUITLESS PURSUITS.

A STRONG MARRIAGE BOND, BLESSED WITH HEALTHY OFFSPRING.

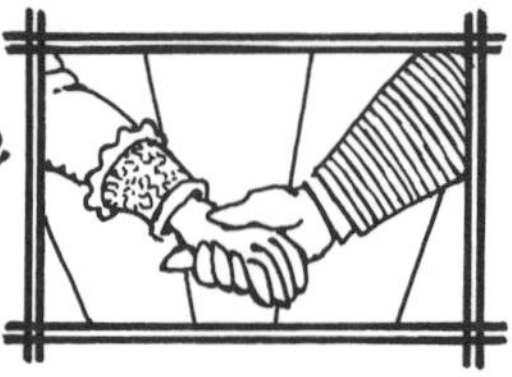

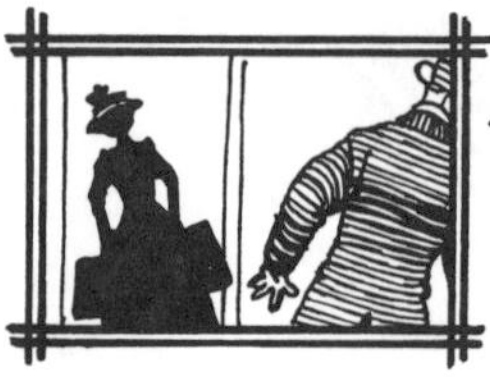

A MARRIAGE BRIEF AND BITTER — SUNDERED BY DIVORCE.

VALOUR ON THE FIELD OF BATTLE.

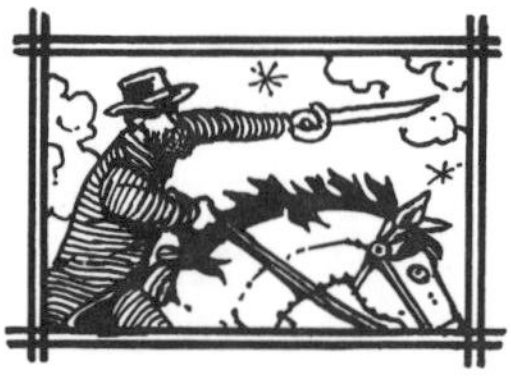

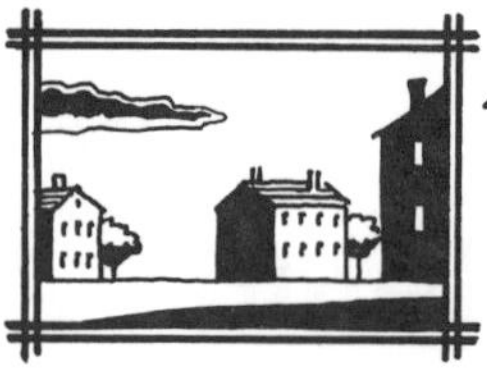

AVOIDANCE OF WAR AT A "RELIGIOUS RETREAT."

A REPUTATION FOR HONESTY, LOYALTY AND FAIR-DEALING TO ALL.

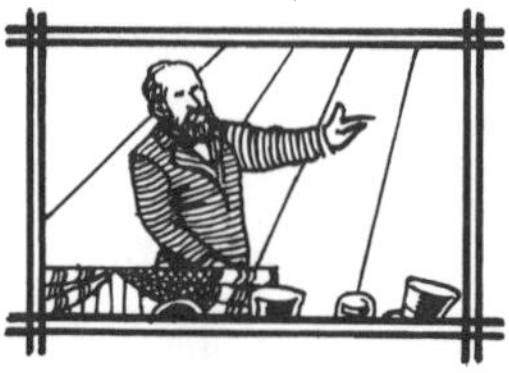

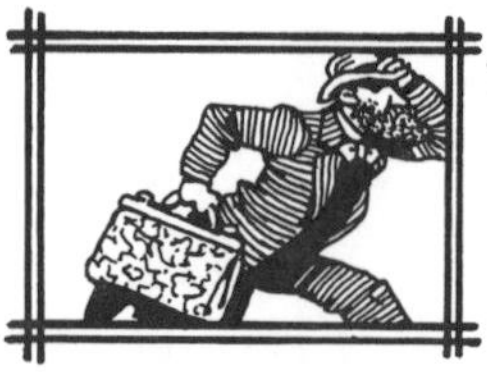

WELL-KNOWN AS CHEAT, CHARLATAN AND HUM-BUG.

A HERO'S BURIAL 'MIDST THE GRIEF OF A NATION.

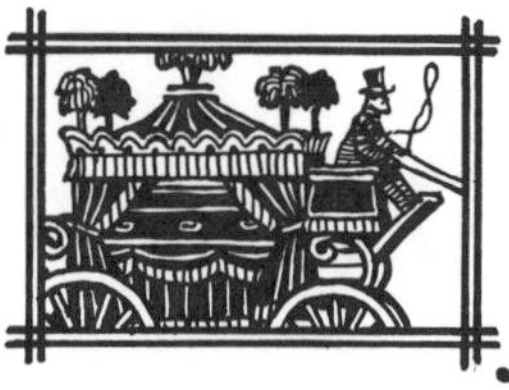

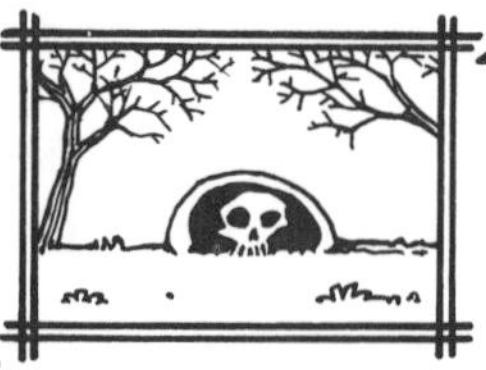

THE WASTE PLACE OF THE DESPISED OUTCAST.

· INTRODUCTORY ·

THE JOURNEY HOME

IN WHICH ARE REVIEWED THE MOURNFUL CEREMONIES OF SEPTEMBER, 1881, AS OUR FALLEN LEADER IS LAID TO HIS REST.

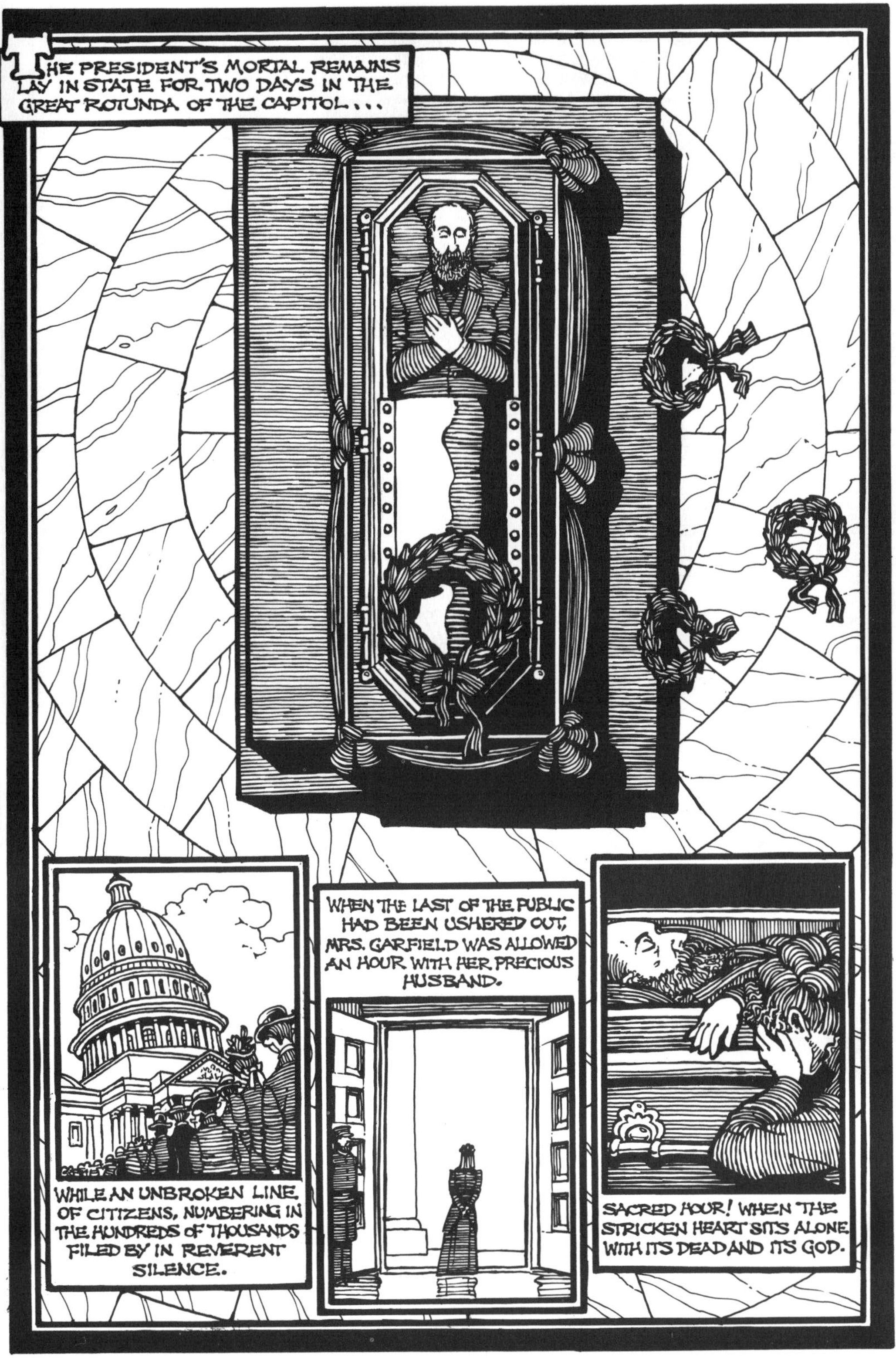
THE PRESIDENT'S MORTAL REMAINS LAY IN STATE FOR TWO DAYS IN THE GREAT ROTUNDA OF THE CAPITOL . . .
WHILE AN UNBROKEN LINE OF CITIZENS, NUMBERING IN THE HUNDREDS OF THOUSANDS FILED BY IN REVERENT SILENCE.
WHEN THE LAST OF THE PUBLIC HAD BEEN USHERED OUT, MRS. GARFIELD WAS ALLOWED AN HOUR WITH HER PRECIOUS HUSBAND.
SACRED HOUR! WHEN THE STRICKEN HEART SITS ALONE WITH ITS DEAD AND ITS GOD.

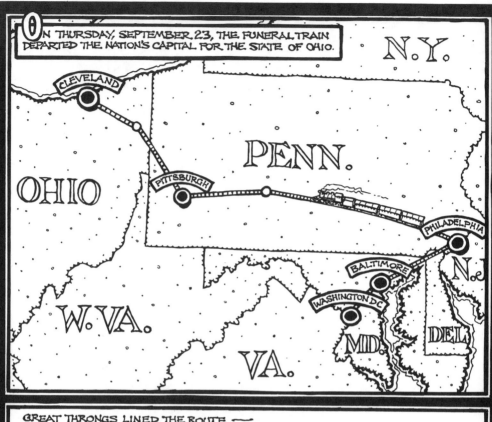

ON THURSDAY, SEPTEMBER 23, THE FUNERAL TRAIN DEPARTED THE NATION'S CAPITAL FOR THE STATE OF OHIO.

N.Y.

CLEVELAND

OHIO

PENN.

PITTSBURGH

PHILADELPHIA

BALTIMORE

N.J.

WASHINGTON D.C.

W. VA.

VA.

MD.

DEL.

GREAT THRONGS LINED THE ROUTE — YOUNG AND OLD, NEGRO AND WHITE, HEADS BARED, BONDED IN MOURNING.

THE WIDOW SAT QUIETLY, GAZING OUT AT THE PASSING SPECTACLE.

THE FARMS ... THE FORESTS ... THE RIVERS ... THE GREAT YOUNG CITIES OF THE BURGEONING HEART-LAND!

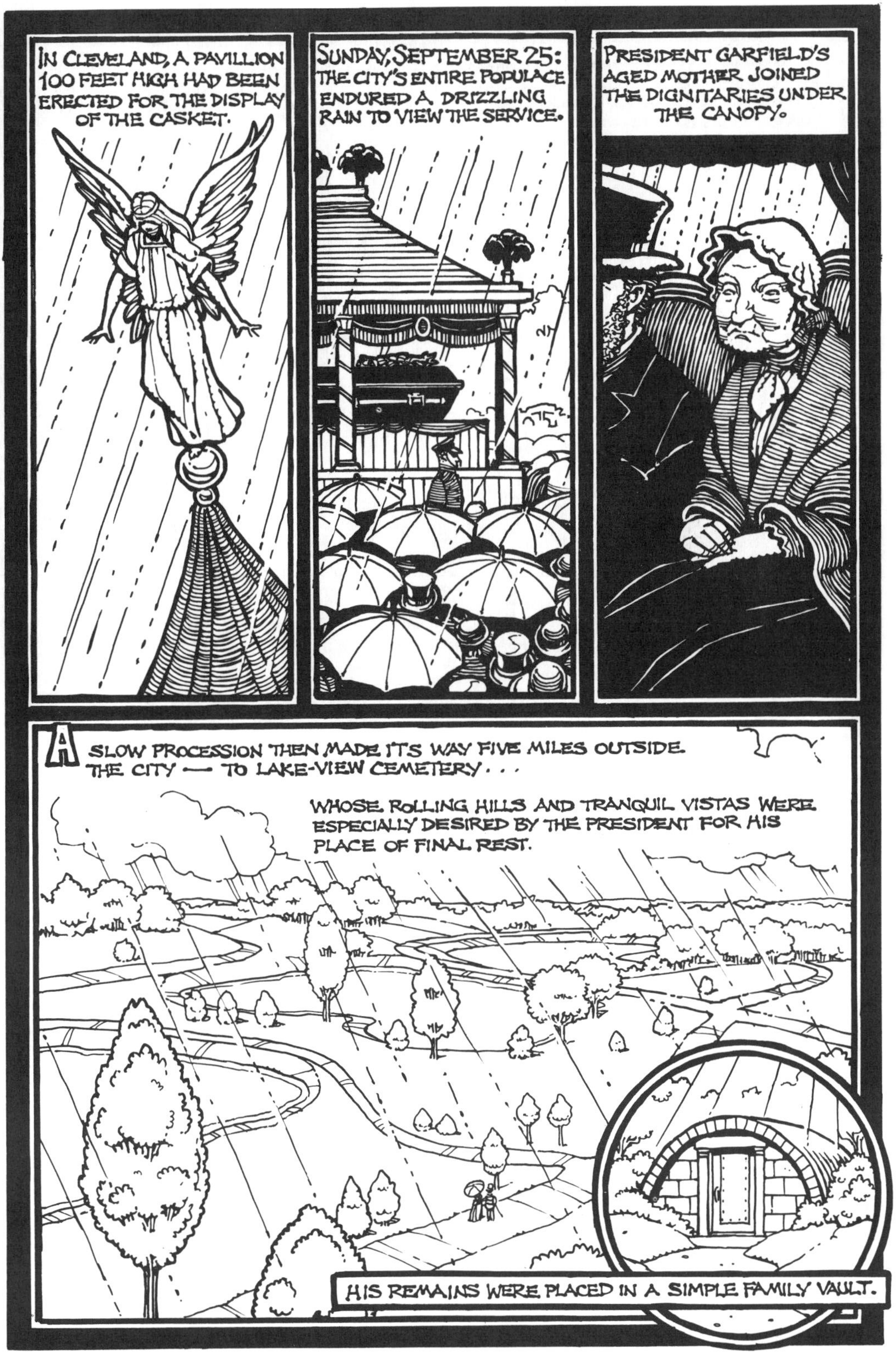
IN CLEVELAND, A PAVILLION 100 FEET HIGH HAD BEEN ERECTED FOR THE DISPLAY OF THE CASKET.
SUNDAY, SEPTEMBER 25: THE CITY'S ENTIRE POPULACE ENDURED A DRIZZLING RAIN TO VIEW THE SERVICE.
PRESIDENT GARFIELD'S AGED MOTHER JOINED THE DIGNITARIES UNDER THE CANOPY.
A SLOW PROCESSION THEN MADE ITS WAY FIVE MILES OUTSIDE THE CITY — TO LAKE-VIEW CEMETERY . . .
WHOSE ROLLING HILLS AND TRANQUIL VISTAS WERE ESPECIALLY DESIRED BY THE PRESIDENT FOR HIS PLACE OF FINAL REST.
HIS REMAINS WERE PLACED IN A SIMPLE FAMILY VAULT.

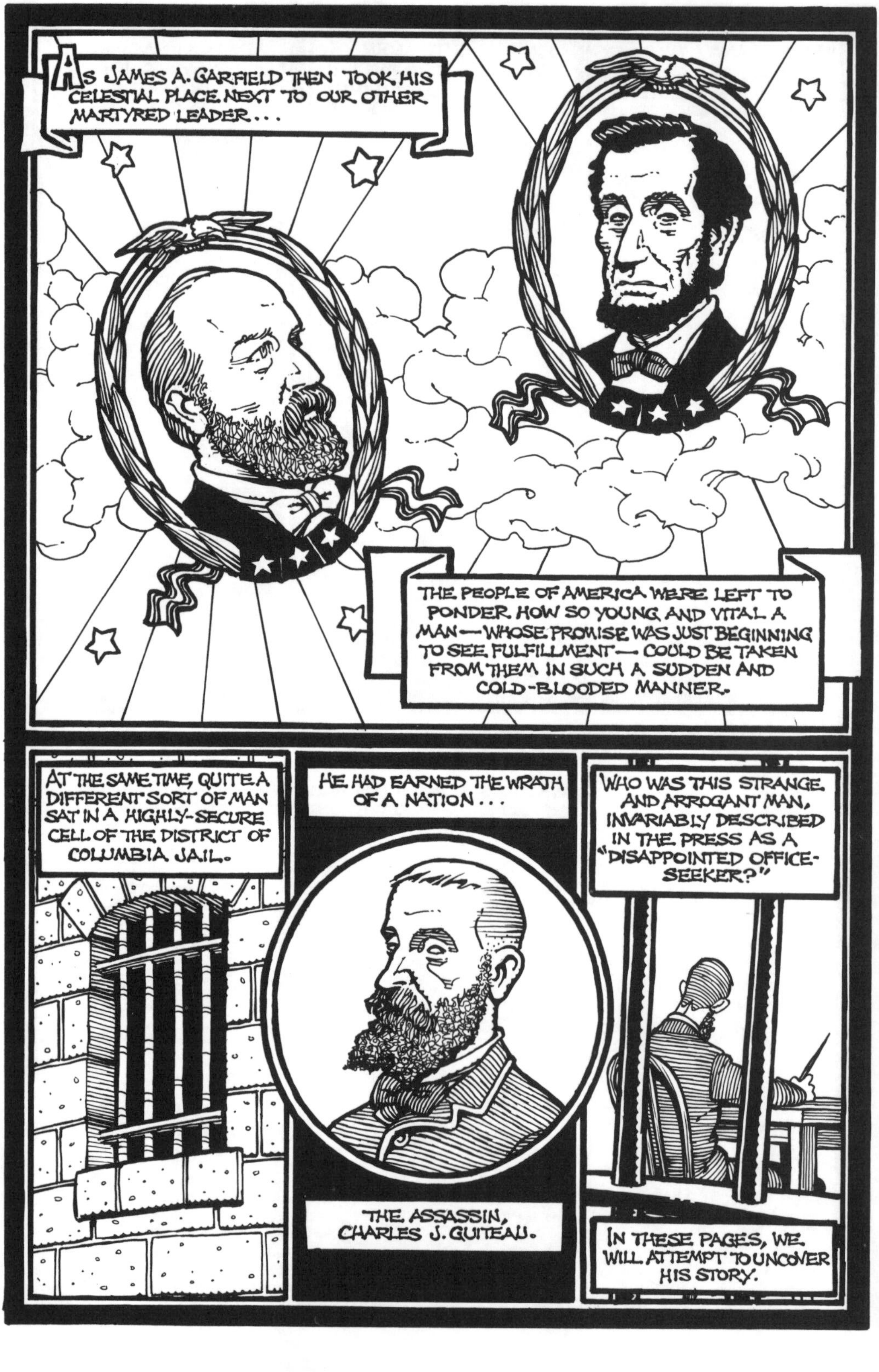
AS JAMES A. GARFIELD THEN TOOK HIS CELESTIAL PLACE NEXT TO OUR OTHER MARTYRED LEADER . . .
THE PEOPLE OF AMERICA WERE LEFT TO PONDER HOW SO YOUNG AND VITAL A MAN — WHOSE PROMISE WAS JUST BEGINNING TO SEE FULFILLMENT — COULD BE TAKEN FROM THEM IN SUCH A SUDDEN AND COLD-BLOODED MANNER.
AT THE SAME TIME, QUITE A DIFFERENT SORT OF MAN SAT IN A HIGHLY-SECURE CELL OF THE DISTRICT OF COLUMBIA JAIL.
HE HAD EARNED THE WRATH OF A NATION . . .
THE ASSASSIN, CHARLES J. GUITEAU.
WHO WAS THIS STRANGE AND ARROGANT MAN, INVARIABLY DESCRIBED IN THE PRESS AS A "DISAPPOINTED OFFICE-SEEKER?"
IN THESE PAGES, WE WILL ATTEMPT TO UNCOVER HIS STORY.

PART I.

PARALLEL LIVES.

IN WHICH WE FOLLOW THE DIVERGENT PATHS OF TWO PRAIRIE-BORN AMERICANS.

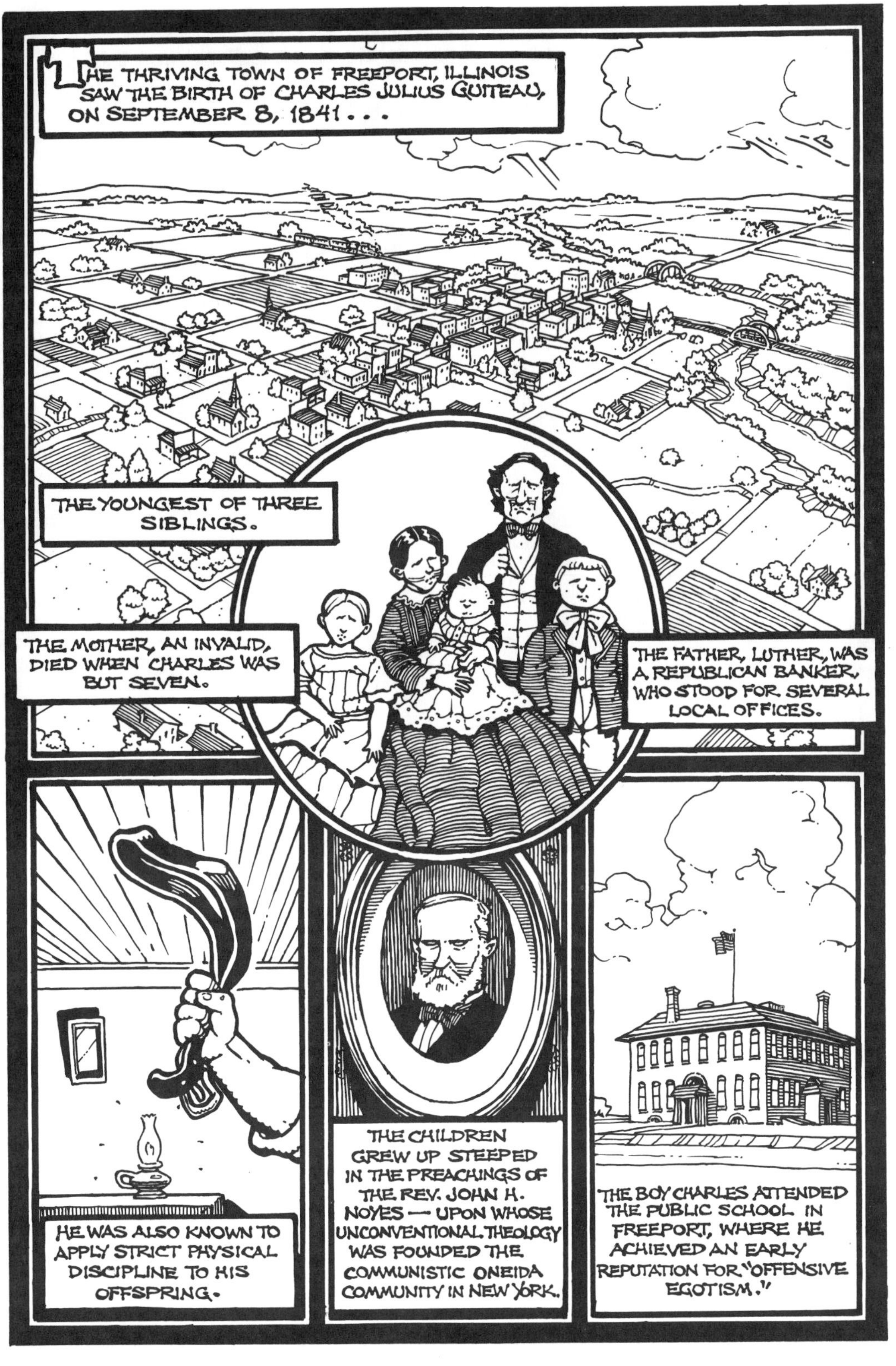
THE THRIVING TOWN OF FREEPORT, ILLINOIS SAW THE BIRTH OF CHARLES JULIUS GUITEAU, ON SEPTEMBER 8, 1841 . . .
THE YOUNGEST OF THREE SIBLINGS.
THE MOTHER, AN INVALID, DIED WHEN CHARLES WAS BUT SEVEN.
THE FATHER, LUTHER, WAS A REPUBLICAN BANKER, WHO STOOD FOR SEVERAL LOCAL OFFICES.
HE WAS ALSO KNOWN TO APPLY STRICT PHYSICAL DISCIPLINE TO HIS OFFSPRING.
THE CHILDREN GREW UP STEEPED IN THE PREACHINGS OF THE REV. JOHN H. NOYES — UPON WHOSE UNCONVENTIONAL THEOLOGY WAS FOUNDED THE COMMUNISTIC ONEIDA COMMUNITY IN NEW YORK.
THE BOY CHARLES ATTENDED THE PUBLIC SCHOOL IN FREEPORT, WHERE HE ACHIEVED AN EARLY REPUTATION FOR "OFFENSIVE EGOTISM."

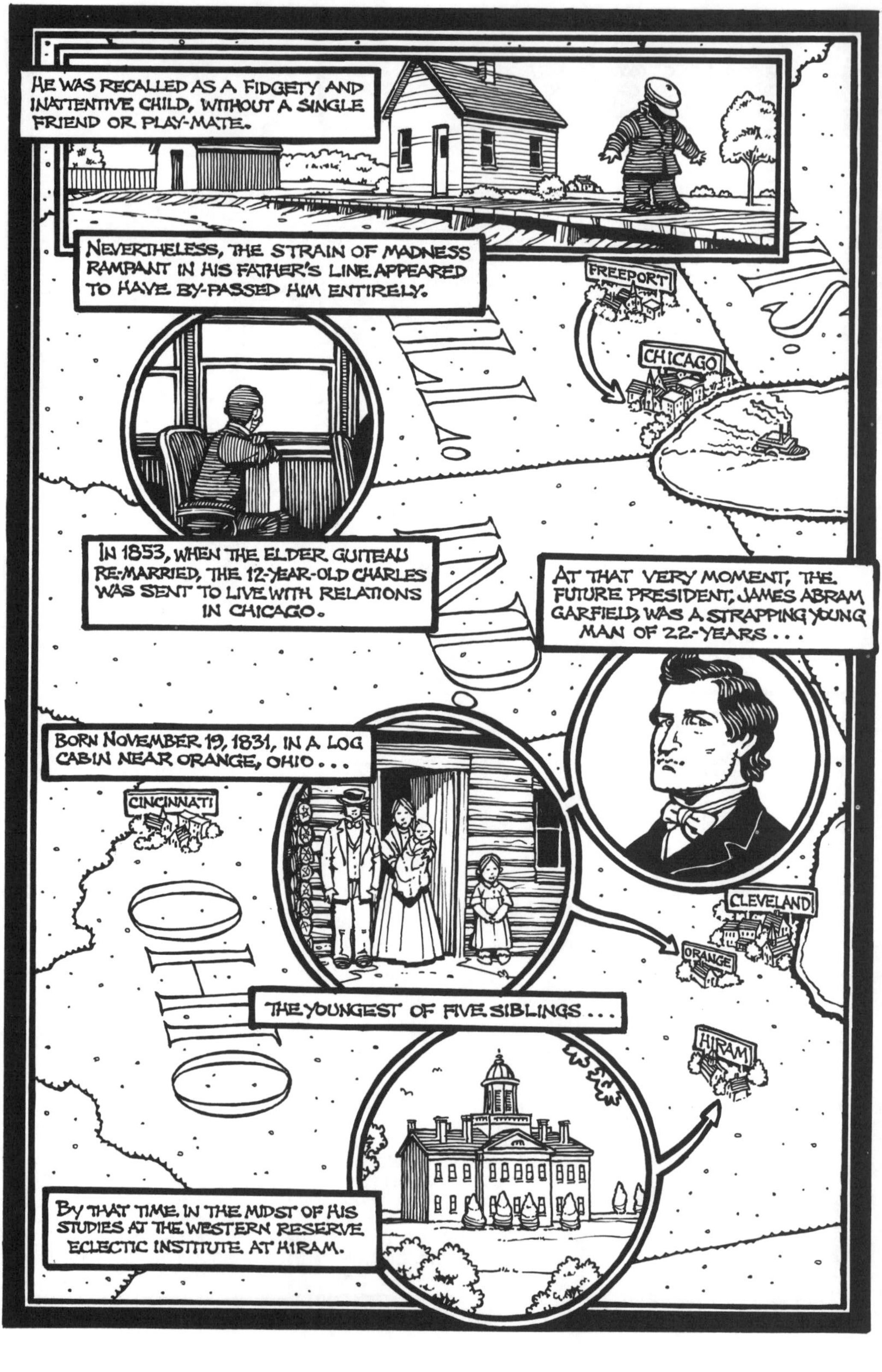
HE WAS RECALLED AS A FIDGETY AND INATTENTIVE CHILD, WITHOUT A SINGLE FRIEND OR PLAY-MATE.
NEVERTHELESS, THE STRAIN OF MADNESS RAMPANT IN HIS FATHER'S LINE APPEARED TO HAVE BY-PASSED HIM ENTIRELY.
FREEPORT
CHICAGO
IN 1853, WHEN THE ELDER GUITEAU RE-MARRIED, THE 12-YEAR-OLD CHARLES WAS SENT TO LIVE WITH RELATIONS IN CHICAGO.
AT THAT VERY MOMENT, THE FUTURE PRESIDENT, JAMES ABRAM GARFIELD, WAS A STRAPPING YOUNG MAN OF 22-YEARS . . .
BORN NOVEMBER 19, 1831, IN A LOG CABIN NEAR ORANGE, OHIO . . .
CINCINNATI
CLEVELAND
ORANGE
THE YOUNGEST OF FIVE SIBLINGS . . .
HIRAM
BY THAT TIME IN THE MIDST OF HIS STUDIES AT THE WESTERN RESERVE ECLECTIC INSTITUTE AT HIRAM.

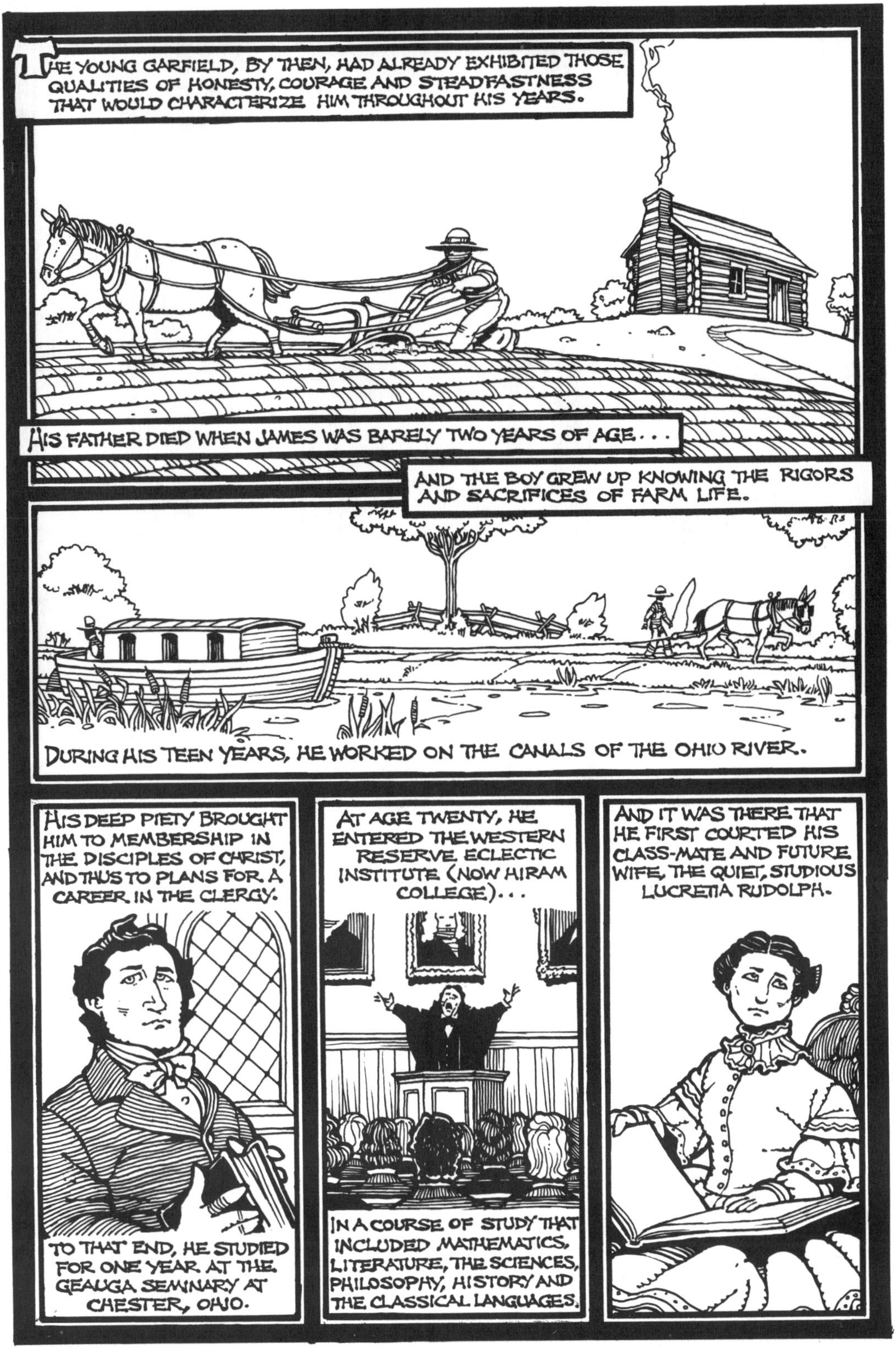
THE YOUNG GARFIELD, BY THEN, HAD ALREADY EXHIBITED THOSE QUALITIES OF HONESTY, COURAGE AND STEADFASTNESS THAT WOULD CHARACTERIZE HIM THROUGHOUT HIS YEARS.
HIS FATHER DIED WHEN JAMES WAS BARELY TWO YEARS OF AGE . . .
AND THE BOY GREW UP KNOWING THE RIGORS AND SACRIFICES OF FARM LIFE.
DURING HIS TEEN YEARS, HE WORKED ON THE CANALS OF THE OHIO RIVER.
HIS DEEP PIETY BROUGHT HIM TO MEMBERSHIP IN THE DISCIPLES OF CHRIST, AND THUS TO PLANS FOR A CAREER IN THE CLERGY.
TO THAT END, HE STUDIED FOR ONE YEAR AT THE GEAUGA SEMINARY AT CHESTER, OHIO.
AT AGE TWENTY, HE ENTERED THE WESTERN RESERVE ECLECTIC INSTITUTE (NOW HIRAM COLLEGE) . . .
IN A COURSE OF STUDY THAT INCLUDED MATHEMATICS, LITERATURE, THE SCIENCES, PHILOSOPHY, HISTORY AND THE CLASSICAL LANGUAGES.
AND IT WAS THERE THAT HE FIRST COURTED HIS CLASS-MATE AND FUTURE WIFE, THE QUIET, STUDIOUS LUCRETIA RUDOLPH.

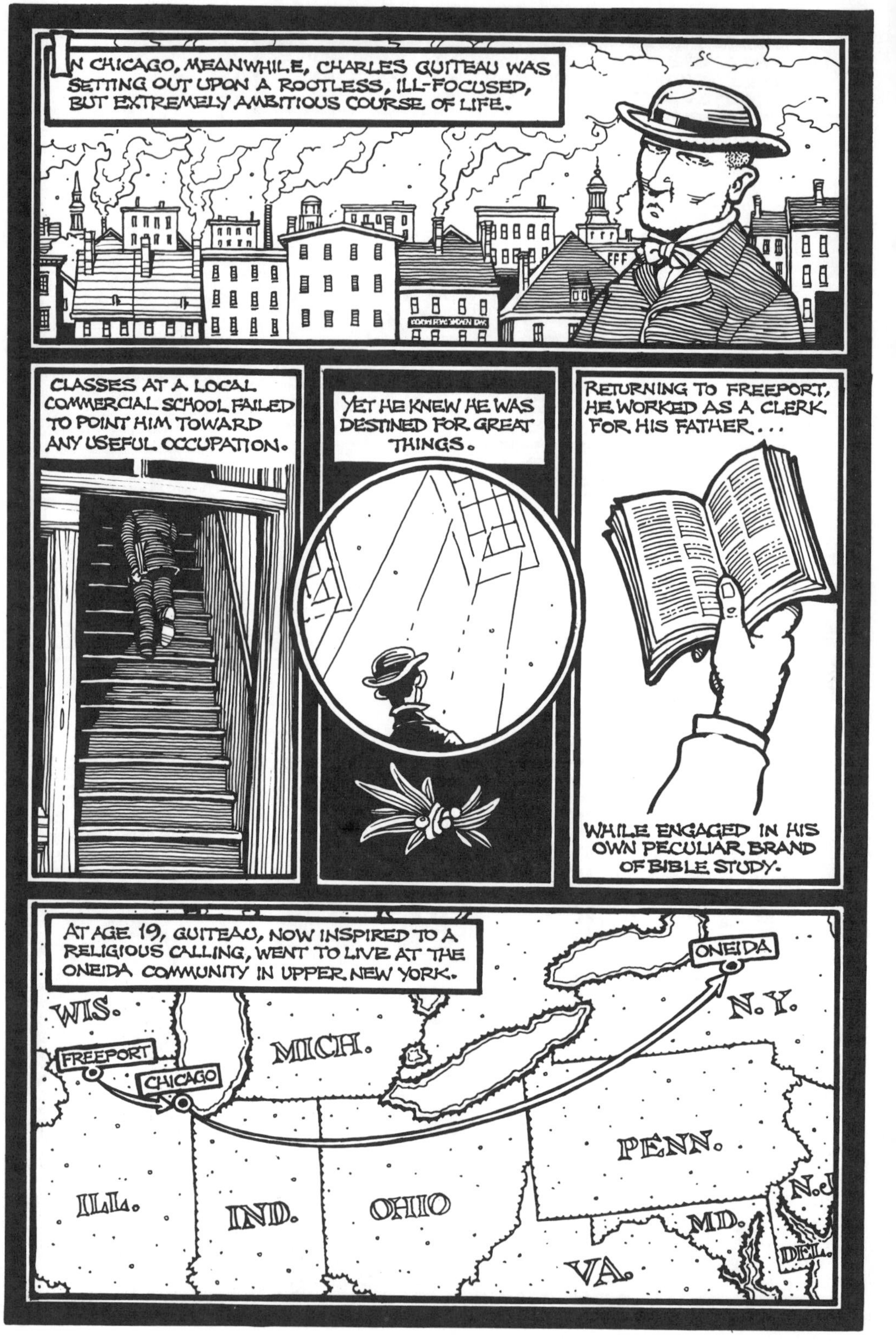
IN CHICAGO, MEANWHILE, CHARLES GUITEAU WAS SETTING OUT UPON A ROOTLESS, ILL-FOCUSED, BUT EXTREMELY AMBITIOUS COURSE OF LIFE.
CLASSES AT A LOCAL COMMERCIAL SCHOOL FAILED TO POINT HIM TOWARD ANY USEFUL OCCUPATION.
YET HE KNEW HE WAS DESTINED FOR GREAT THINGS.
RETURNING TO FREEPORT, HE WORKED AS A CLERK FOR HIS FATHER . . .
WHILE ENGAGED IN HIS OWN PECULIAR BRAND OF BIBLE STUDY.
AT AGE 19, GUITEAU, NOW INSPIRED TO A RELIGIOUS CALLING, WENT TO LIVE AT THE ONEIDA COMMUNITY IN UPPER NEW YORK.
ONEIDA
WIS.
N.Y.
MICH.
FREEPORT
CHICAGO
PENN.
ILL.
IND.
OHIO
N.J.
MD.
DEL.
VA.

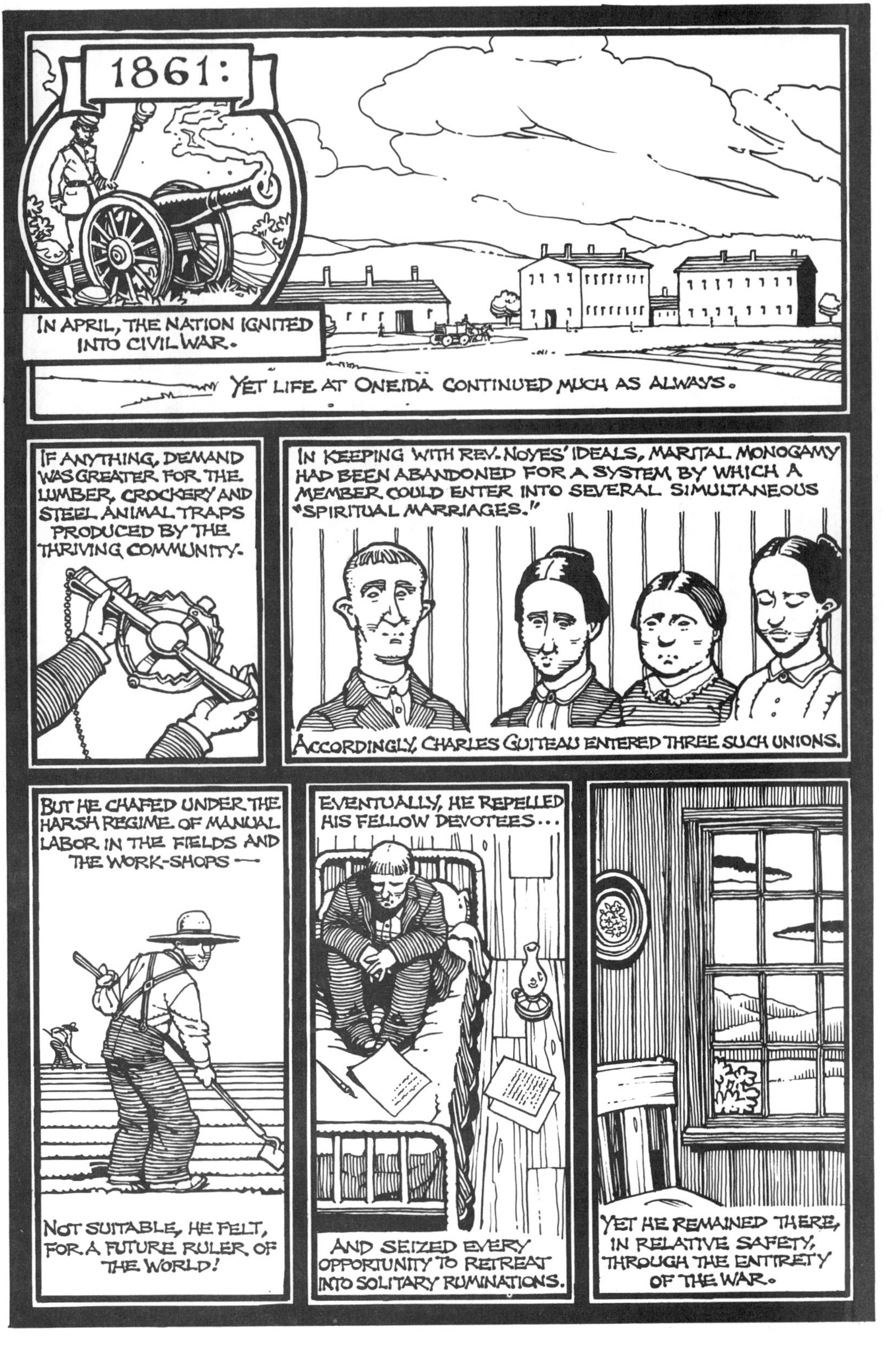
1861:
IN APRIL, THE NATION IGNITED INTO CIVIL WAR.
YET LIFE AT ONEIDA CONTINUED MUCH AS ALWAYS.
IF ANYTHING, DEMAND WAS GREATER FOR THE LUMBER, CROCKERY AND STEEL ANIMAL TRAPS PRODUCED BY THE THRIVING COMMUNITY.
IN KEEPING WITH REV. NOYES' IDEALS, MARITAL MONOGAMY HAD BEEN ABANDONED FOR A SYSTEM BY WHICH A MEMBER COULD ENTER INTO SEVERAL SIMULTANEOUS "SPIRITUAL MARRIAGES."
ACCORDINGLY, CHARLES GUITEAU ENTERED THREE SUCH UNIONS.
BUT HE CHAFED UNDER THE HARSH REGIME OF MANUAL LABOR IN THE FIELDS AND THE WORK-SHOPS —
NOT SUITABLE, HE FELT, FOR A FUTURE RULER OF THE WORLD!
EVENTUALLY, HE REPELLED HIS FELLOW DEVOTEES...
AND SEIZED EVERY OPPORTUNITY TO RETREAT INTO SOLITARY RUMINATIONS.
YET HE REMAINED THERE, IN RELATIVE SAFETY, THROUGH THE ENTIRETY OF THE WAR.

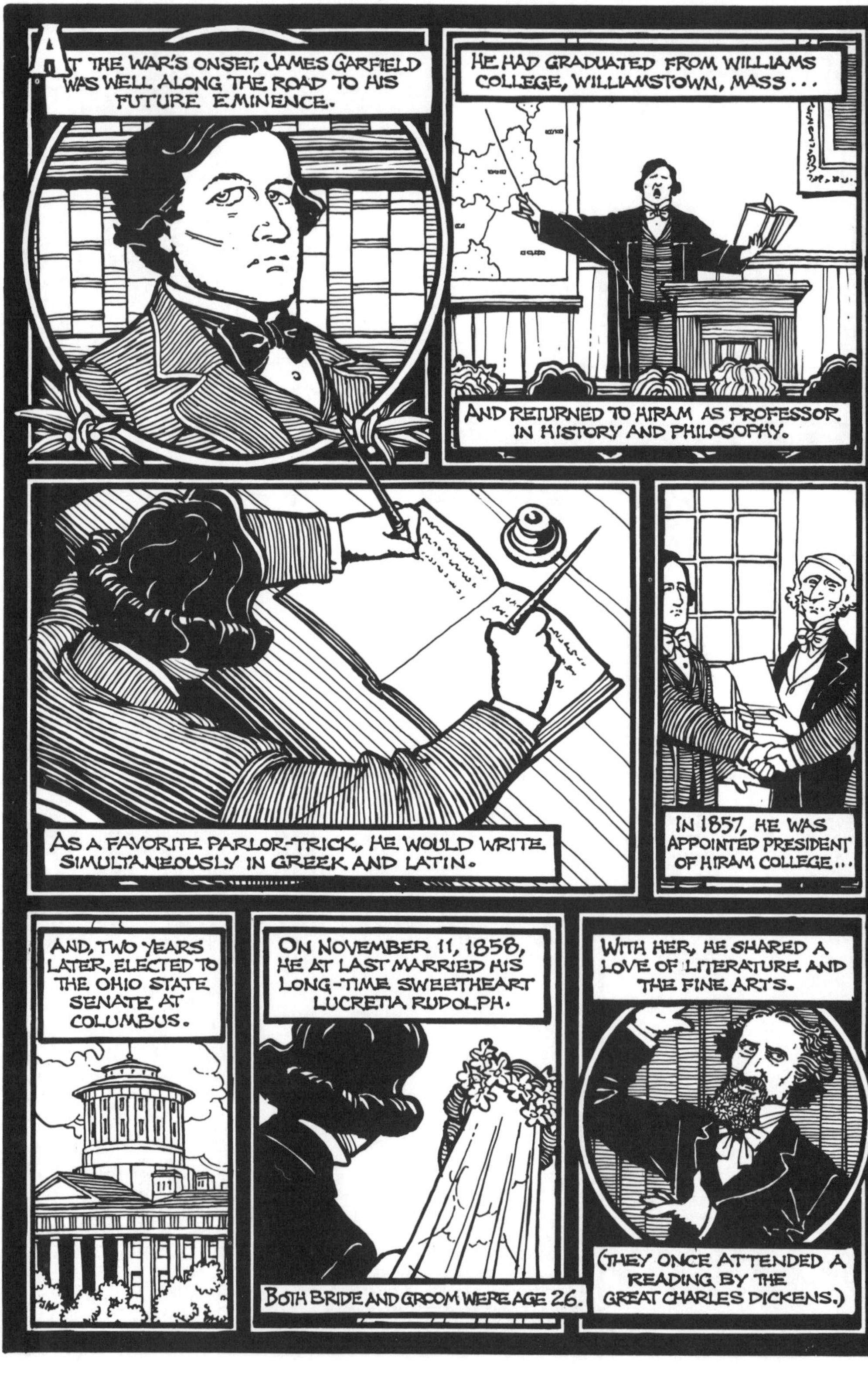
AT THE WAR'S ONSET, JAMES GARFIELD WAS WELL ALONG THE ROAD TO HIS FUTURE EMINENCE.
HE HAD GRADUATED FROM WILLIAMS COLLEGE, WILLIAMSTOWN, MASS...
AND RETURNED TO HIRAM AS PROFESSOR IN HISTORY AND PHILOSOPHY.
AS A FAVORITE PARLOR-TRICK, HE WOULD WRITE SIMULTANEOUSLY IN GREEK AND LATIN.
IN 1857, HE WAS APPOINTED PRESIDENT OF HIRAM COLLEGE...
AND, TWO YEARS LATER, ELECTED TO THE OHIO STATE SENATE AT COLUMBUS.
ON NOVEMBER 11, 1858, HE AT LAST MARRIED HIS LONG-TIME SWEETHEART LUCRETIA RUDOLPH.
BOTH BRIDE AND GROOM WERE AGE 26.
WITH HER, HE SHARED A LOVE OF LITERATURE AND THE FINE ARTS.
(THEY ONCE ATTENDED A READING BY THE GREAT CHARLES DICKENS.)

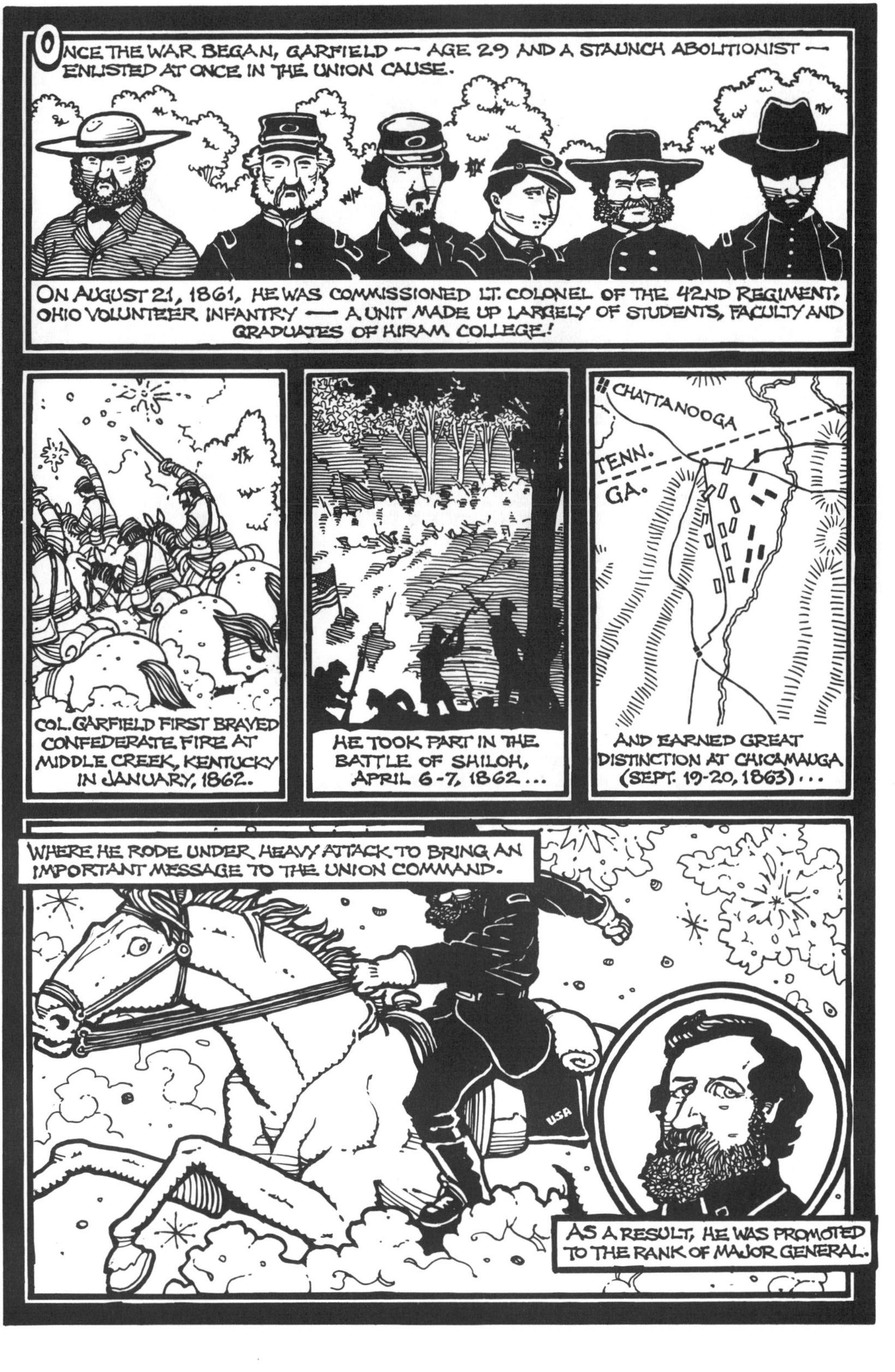
ONCE THE WAR BEGAN, GARFIELD — AGE 29 AND A STAUNCH ABOLITIONIST — ENLISTED AT ONCE IN THE UNION CAUSE.
ON AUGUST 21, 1861, HE WAS COMMISSIONED LT. COLONEL OF THE 42ND REGIMENT, OHIO VOLUNTEER INFANTRY — A UNIT MADE UP LARGELY OF STUDENTS, FACULTY AND GRADUATES OF HIRAM COLLEGE!
COL. GARFIELD FIRST BRAVED CONFEDERATE FIRE AT MIDDLE CREEK, KENTUCKY IN JANUARY, 1862.
HE TOOK PART IN THE BATTLE OF SHILOH, APRIL 6-7, 1862...
CHATTANOOGA
TENN.
GA.
AND EARNED GREAT DISTINCTION AT CHICAMAUGA (SEPT. 19-20, 1863)...
WHERE HE RODE UNDER HEAVY ATTACK TO BRING AN IMPORTANT MESSAGE TO THE UNION COMMAND.
USA
AS A RESULT, HE WAS PROMOTED TO THE RANK OF MAJOR GENERAL.

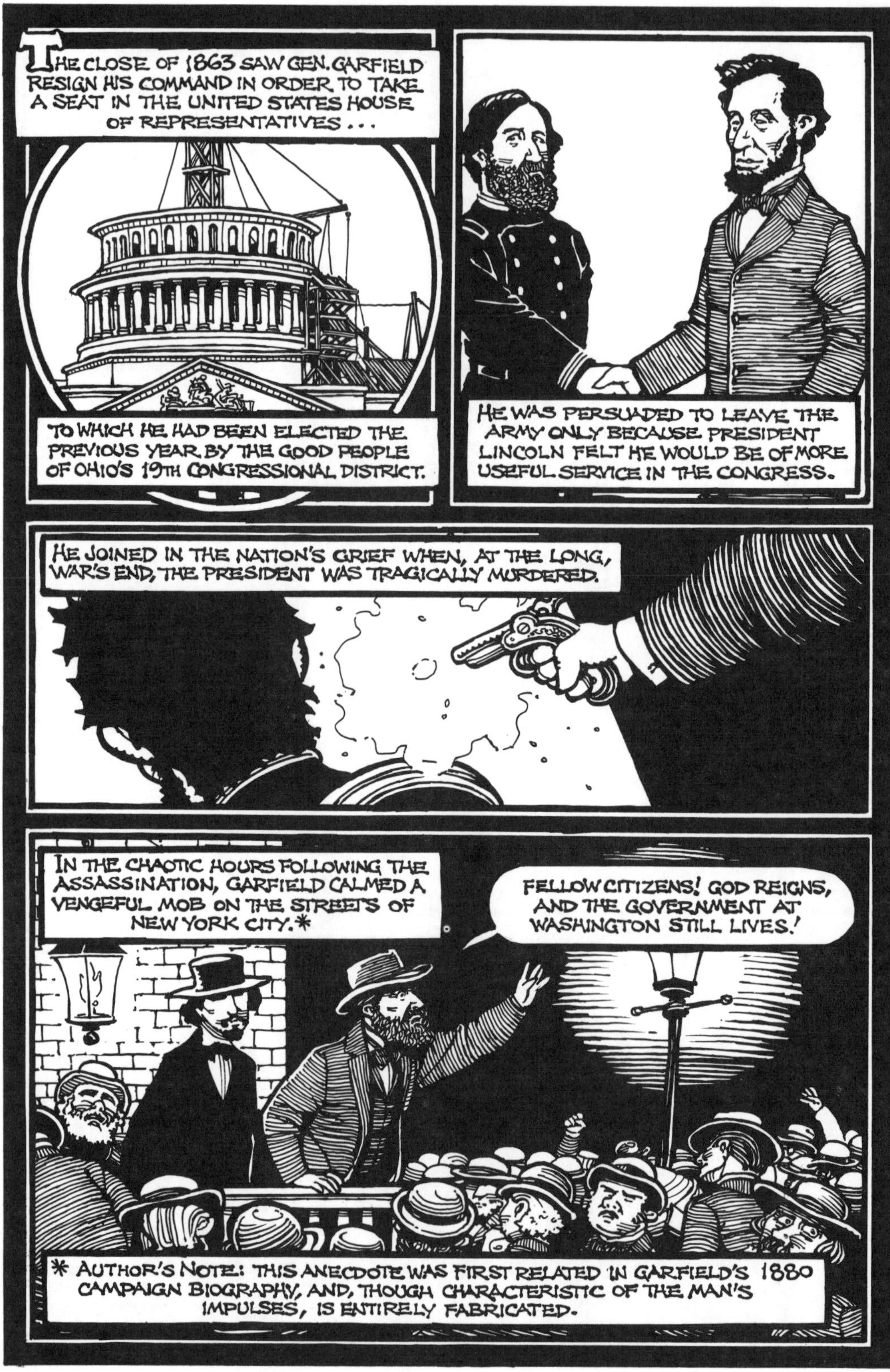
THE CLOSE OF 1863 SAW GEN. GARFIELD RESIGN HIS COMMAND IN ORDER TO TAKE A SEAT IN THE UNITED STATES HOUSE OF REPRESENTATIVES . . .
TO WHICH HE HAD BEEN ELECTED THE PREVIOUS YEAR BY THE GOOD PEOPLE OF OHIO'S 19TH CONGRESSIONAL DISTRICT.
HE WAS PERSUADED TO LEAVE THE ARMY ONLY BECAUSE PRESIDENT LINCOLN FELT HE WOULD BE OF MORE USEFUL SERVICE IN THE CONGRESS.
HE JOINED IN THE NATION'S GRIEF WHEN, AT THE LONG WAR'S END, THE PRESIDENT WAS TRAGICALLY MURDERED.
IN THE CHAOTIC HOURS FOLLOWING THE ASSASSINATION, GARFIELD CALMED A VENGEFUL MOB ON THE STREETS OF NEW YORK CITY.*
FELLOW CITIZENS! GOD REIGNS, AND THE GOVERNMENT AT WASHINGTON STILL LIVES!
* AUTHOR'S NOTE: THIS ANECDOTE WAS FIRST RELATED IN GARFIELD'S 1880 CAMPAIGN BIOGRAPHY, AND, THOUGH CHARACTERISTIC OF THE MAN'S IMPULSES, IS ENTIRELY FABRICATED.

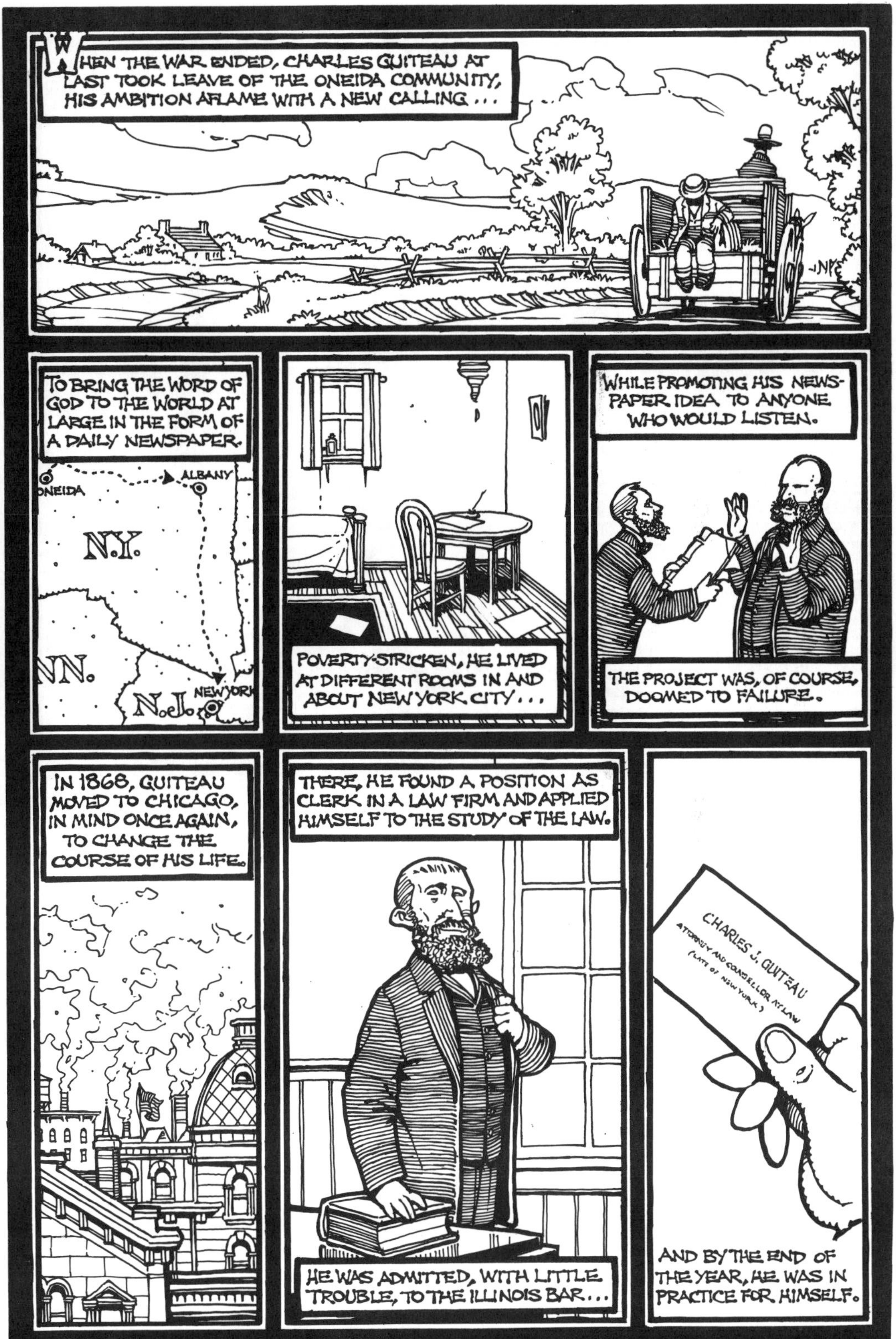
WHEN THE WAR ENDED, CHARLES GUITEAU AT LAST TOOK LEAVE OF THE ONEIDA COMMUNITY, HIS AMBITION AFLAME WITH A NEW CALLING . . .
TO BRING THE WORD OF GOD TO THE WORLD AT LARGE IN THE FORM OF A DAILY NEWSPAPER.
ONEIDA
ALBANY
N.Y.
N.J.
NEW YORK
POVERTY-STRICKEN, HE LIVED AT DIFFERENT ROOMS IN AND ABOUT NEW YORK CITY . . .
WHILE PROMOTING HIS NEWSPAPER IDEA TO ANYONE WHO WOULD LISTEN.
THE PROJECT WAS, OF COURSE, DOOMED TO FAILURE.
IN 1868, GUITEAU MOVED TO CHICAGO, IN MIND ONCE AGAIN, TO CHANGE THE COURSE OF HIS LIFE.
THERE, HE FOUND A POSITION AS CLERK IN A LAW FIRM AND APPLIED HIMSELF TO THE STUDY OF THE LAW.
HE WAS ADMITTED, WITH LITTLE TROUBLE, TO THE ILLINOIS BAR . . .
CHARLES J. GUITEAU
ATTORNEY AND COUNSELLOR AT LAW
(LATE OF NEW YORK)
AND BY THE END OF THE YEAR, HE WAS IN PRACTICE FOR HIMSELF.

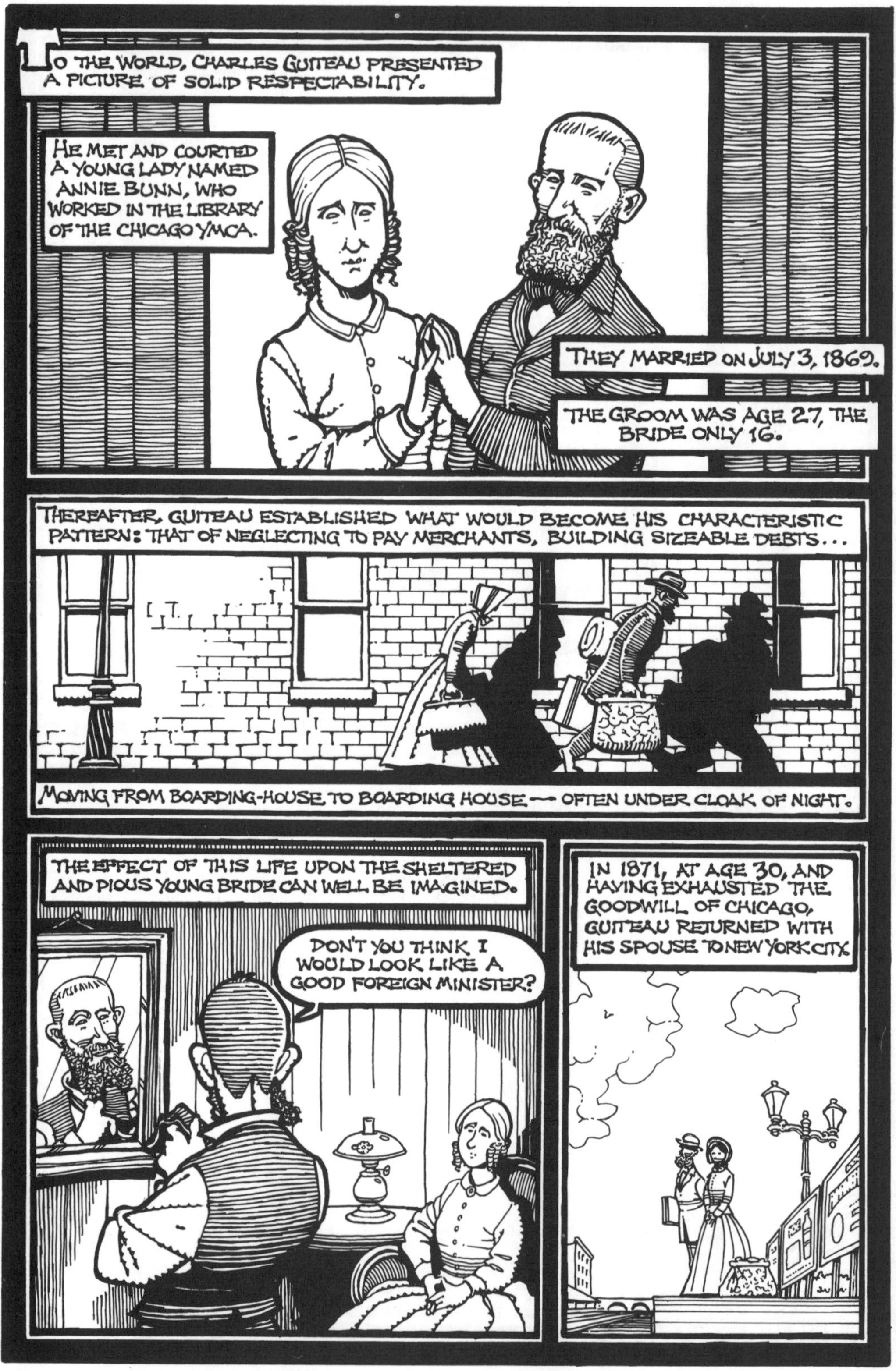
TO THE WORLD, CHARLES GUITEAU PRESENTED A PICTURE OF SOLID RESPECTABILITY.
HE MET AND COURTED A YOUNG LADY NAMED ANNIE BUNN, WHO WORKED IN THE LIBRARY OF THE CHICAGO YMCA.
THEY MARRIED ON JULY 3, 1869.
THE GROOM WAS AGE 27, THE BRIDE ONLY 16.
THEREAFTER, GUITEAU ESTABLISHED WHAT WOULD BECOME HIS CHARACTERISTIC PATTERN: THAT OF NEGLECTING TO PAY MERCHANTS, BUILDING SIZEABLE DEBTS...
MOVING FROM BOARDING-HOUSE TO BOARDING HOUSE — OFTEN UNDER CLOAK OF NIGHT.
THE EFFECT OF THIS LIFE UPON THE SHELTERED AND PIOUS YOUNG BRIDE CAN WELL BE IMAGINED.
DON'T YOU THINK I WOULD LOOK LIKE A GOOD FOREIGN MINISTER?
IN 1871, AT AGE 30, AND HAVING EXHAUSTED THE GOODWILL OF CHICAGO, GUITEAU RETURNED WITH HIS SPOUSE TO NEW YORK CITY.

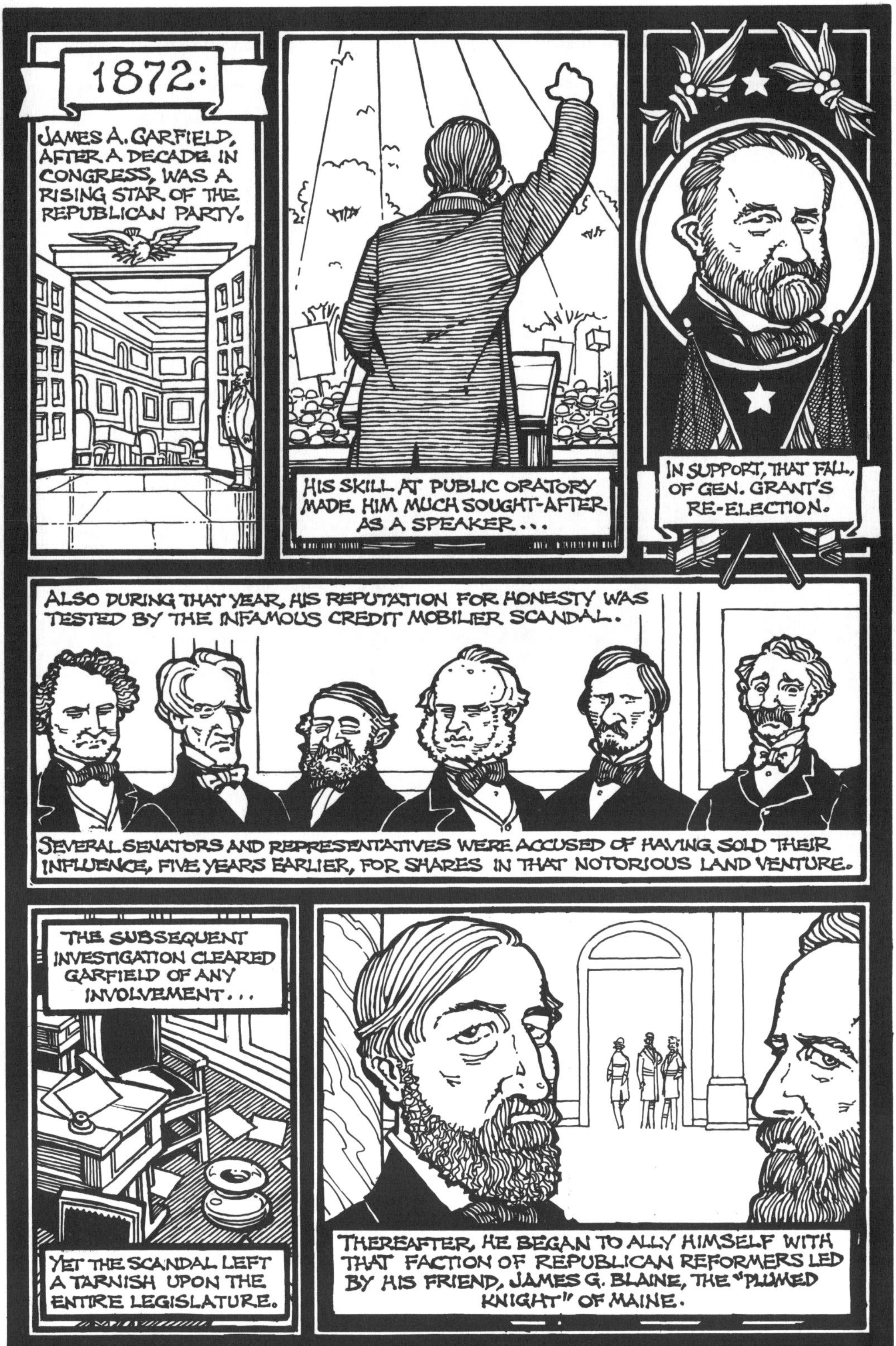
1872:
JAMES A. GARFIELD, AFTER A DECADE IN CONGRESS, WAS A RISING STAR OF THE REPUBLICAN PARTY.
HIS SKILL AT PUBLIC ORATORY MADE HIM MUCH SOUGHT-AFTER AS A SPEAKER...
IN SUPPORT, THAT FALL, OF GEN. GRANT'S RE-ELECTION.
ALSO DURING THAT YEAR, HIS REPUTATION FOR HONESTY WAS TESTED BY THE INFAMOUS CREDIT MOBILIER SCANDAL.
SEVERAL SENATORS AND REPRESENTATIVES WERE ACCUSED OF HAVING SOLD THEIR INFLUENCE, FIVE YEARS EARLIER, FOR SHARES IN THAT NOTORIOUS LAND VENTURE.
THE SUBSEQUENT INVESTIGATION CLEARED GARFIELD OF ANY INVOLVEMENT...
YET THE SCANDAL LEFT A TARNISH UPON THE ENTIRE LEGISLATURE.
THEREAFTER, HE BEGAN TO ALLY HIMSELF WITH THAT FACTION OF REPUBLICAN REFORMERS LED BY HIS FRIEND, JAMES G. BLAINE, THE "PLUMED KNIGHT" OF MAINE.

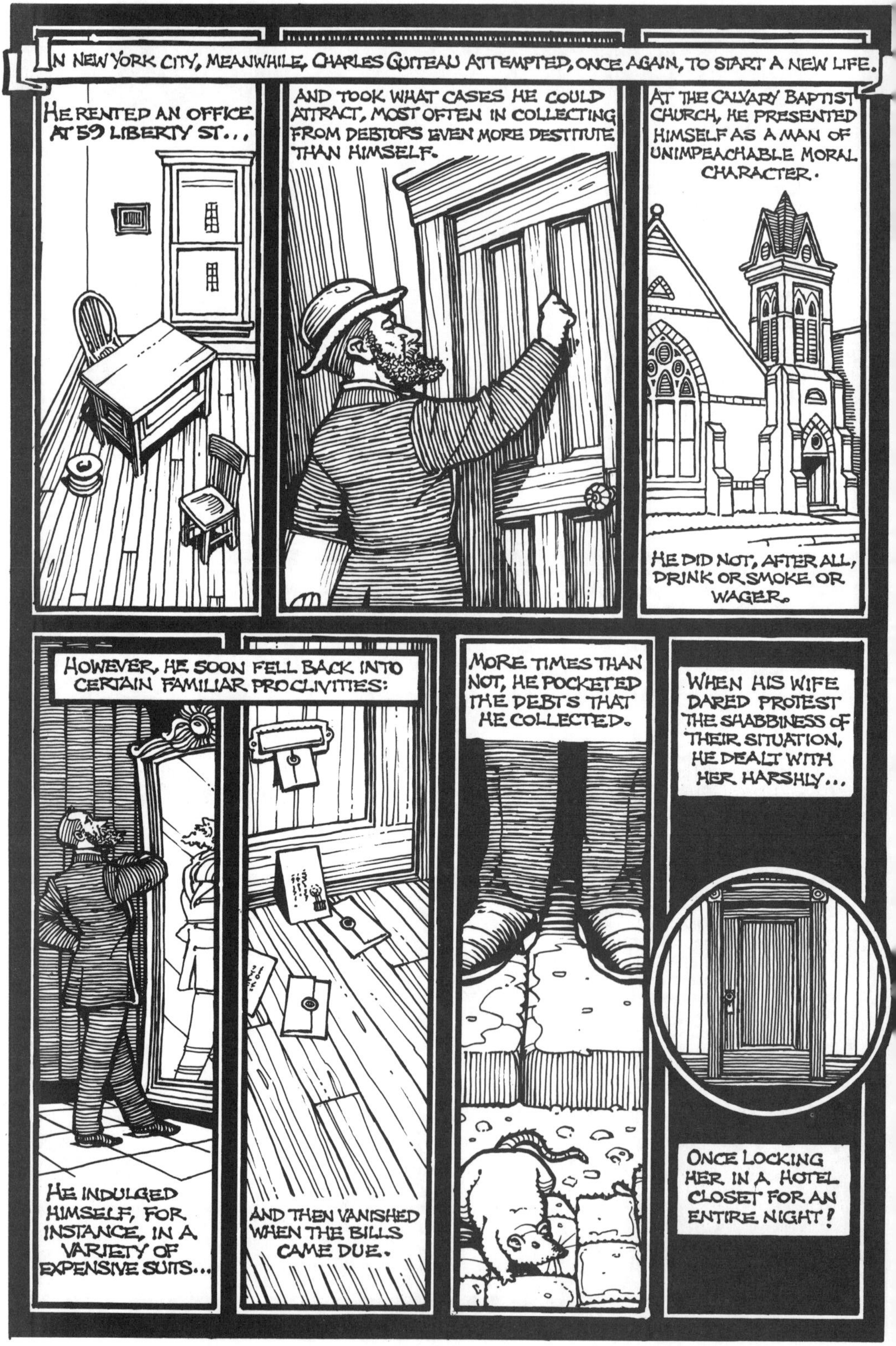
IN NEW YORK CITY, MEANWHILE, CHARLES GUITEAU ATTEMPTED, ONCE AGAIN, TO START A NEW LIFE.
HE RENTED AN OFFICE AT 59 LIBERTY ST...
AND TOOK WHAT CASES HE COULD ATTRACT, MOST OFTEN IN COLLECTING FROM DEBTORS EVEN MORE DESTITUTE THAN HIMSELF.
AT THE CALVARY BAPTIST CHURCH, HE PRESENTED HIMSELF AS A MAN OF UNIMPEACHABLE MORAL CHARACTER.
HE DID NOT, AFTER ALL, DRINK OR SMOKE OR WAGER.
HOWEVER, HE SOON FELL BACK INTO CERTAIN FAMILIAR PROCLIVITIES:
HE INDULGED HIMSELF, FOR INSTANCE, IN A VARIETY OF EXPENSIVE SUITS...
AND THEN VANISHED WHEN THE BILLS CAME DUE.
MORE TIMES THAN NOT, HE POCKETED THE DEBTS THAT HE COLLECTED.
WHEN HIS WIFE DARED PROTEST THE SHABBINESS OF THEIR SITUATION, HE DEALT WITH HER HARSHLY...
ONCE LOCKING HER IN A HOTEL CLOSET FOR AN ENTIRE NIGHT!

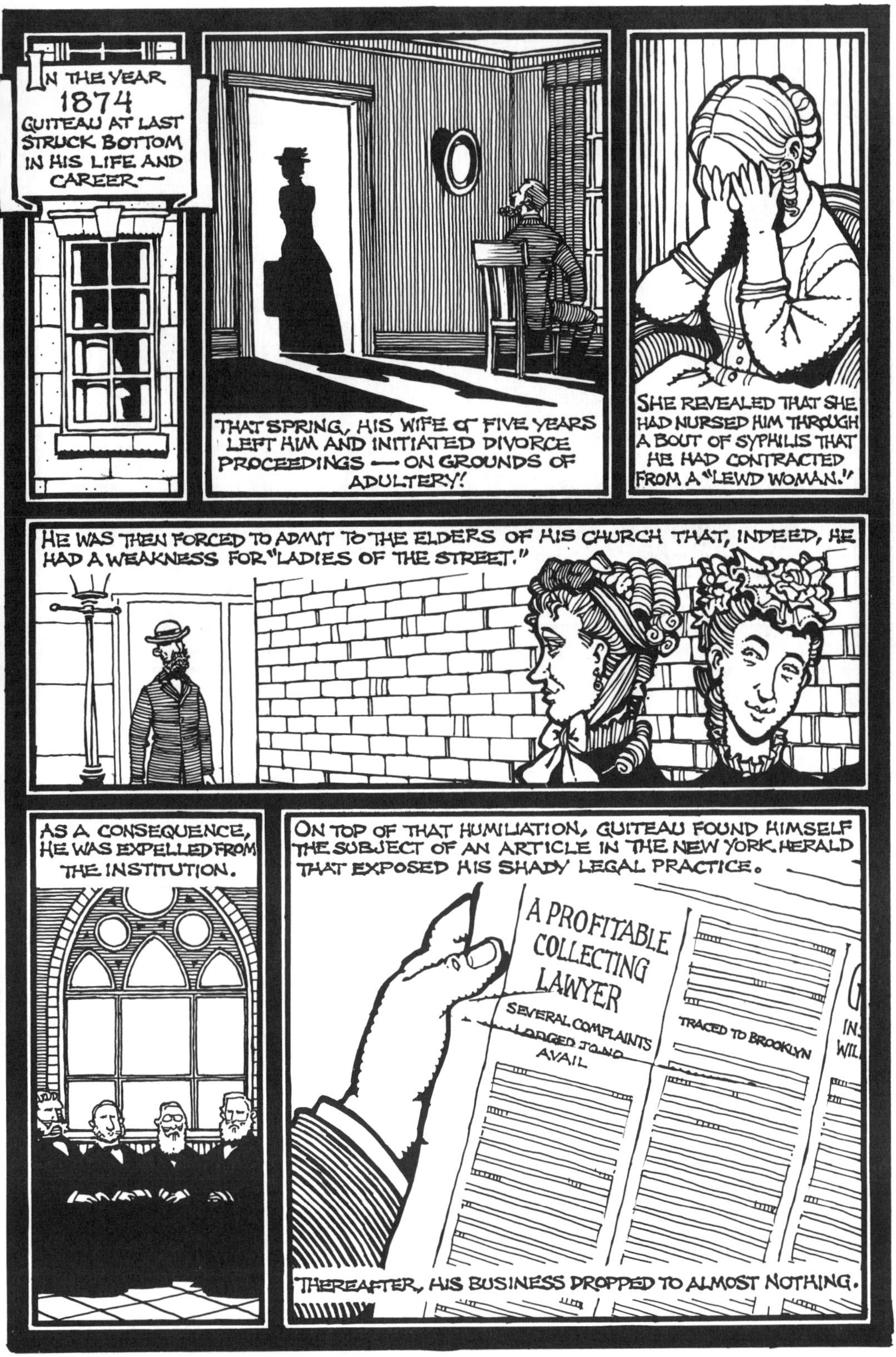
IN THE YEAR 1874 GUITEAU AT LAST STRUCK BOTTOM IN HIS LIFE AND CAREER—
THAT SPRING, HIS WIFE OF FIVE YEARS LEFT HIM AND INITIATED DIVORCE PROCEEDINGS — ON GROUNDS OF ADULTERY!
SHE REVEALED THAT SHE HAD NURSED HIM THROUGH A BOUT OF SYPHILIS THAT HE HAD CONTRACTED FROM A "LEWD WOMAN."
HE WAS THEN FORCED TO ADMIT TO THE ELDERS OF HIS CHURCH THAT, INDEED, HE HAD A WEAKNESS FOR "LADIES OF THE STREET."
AS A CONSEQUENCE, HE WAS EXPELLED FROM THE INSTITUTION.
ON TOP OF THAT HUMILIATION, GUITEAU FOUND HIMSELF THE SUBJECT OF AN ARTICLE IN THE NEW YORK HERALD THAT EXPOSED HIS SHADY LEGAL PRACTICE.
A PROFITABLE COLLECTING LAWYER
SEVERAL COMPLAINTS LODGED TO NO AVAIL
TRACED TO BROOKLYN
THEREAFTER, HIS BUSINESS DROPPED TO ALMOST NOTHING.

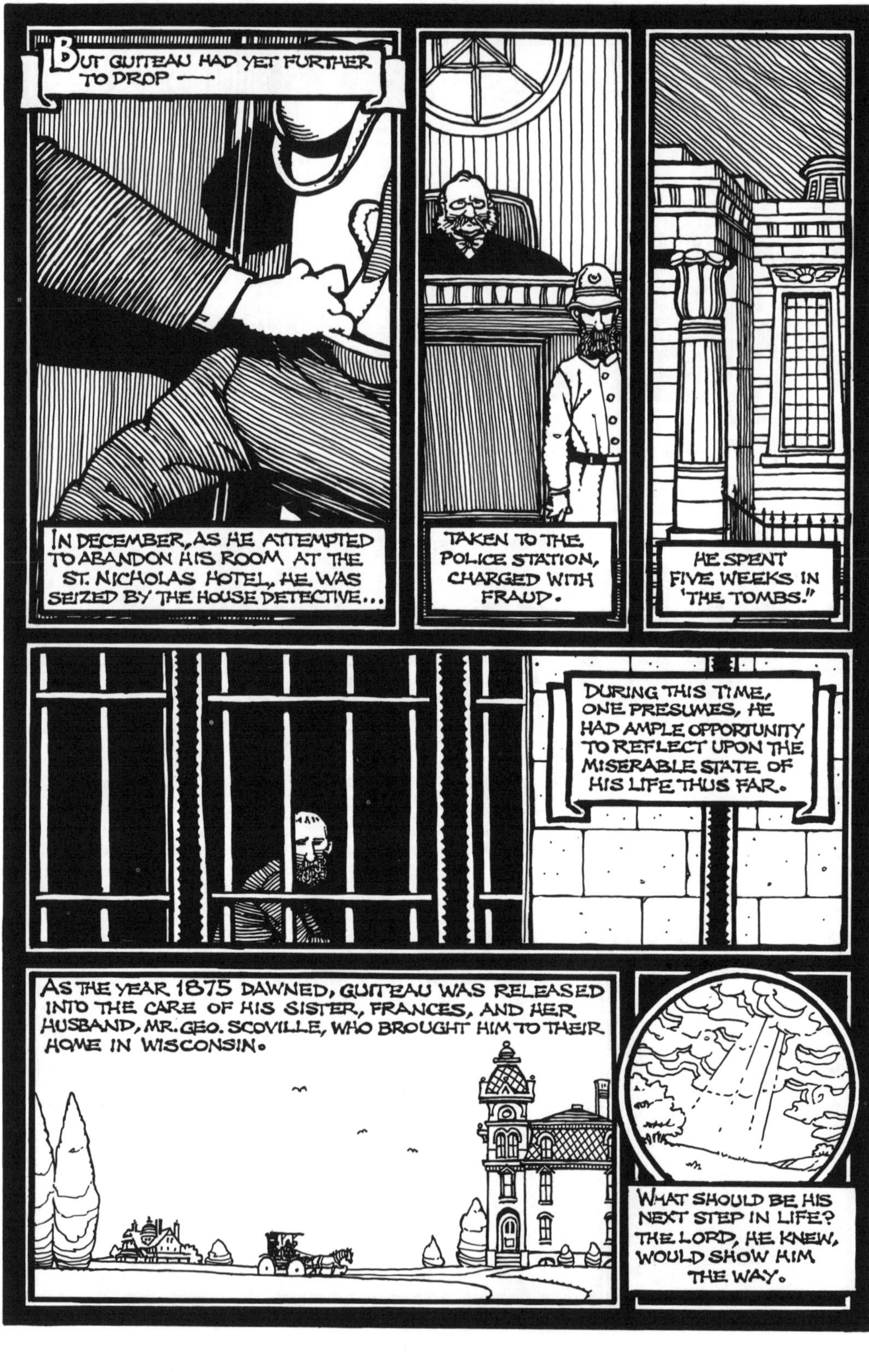

BUT GUITEAU HAD YET FURTHER TO DROP —
IN DECEMBER, AS HE ATTEMPTED TO ABANDON HIS ROOM AT THE ST. NICHOLAS HOTEL, HE WAS SEIZED BY THE HOUSE DETECTIVE...
TAKEN TO THE POLICE STATION, CHARGED WITH FRAUD.
HE SPENT FIVE WEEKS IN 'THE TOMBS.'
DURING THIS TIME, ONE PRESUMES, HE HAD AMPLE OPPORTUNITY TO REFLECT UPON THE MISERABLE STATE OF HIS LIFE THUS FAR.
AS THE YEAR 1875 DAWNED, GUITEAU WAS RELEASED INTO THE CARE OF HIS SISTER, FRANCES, AND HER HUSBAND, MR. GEO. SCOVILLE, WHO BROUGHT HIM TO THEIR HOME IN WISCONSIN.
WHAT SHOULD BE HIS NEXT STEP IN LIFE? THE LORD, HE KNEW, WOULD SHOW HIM THE WAY.

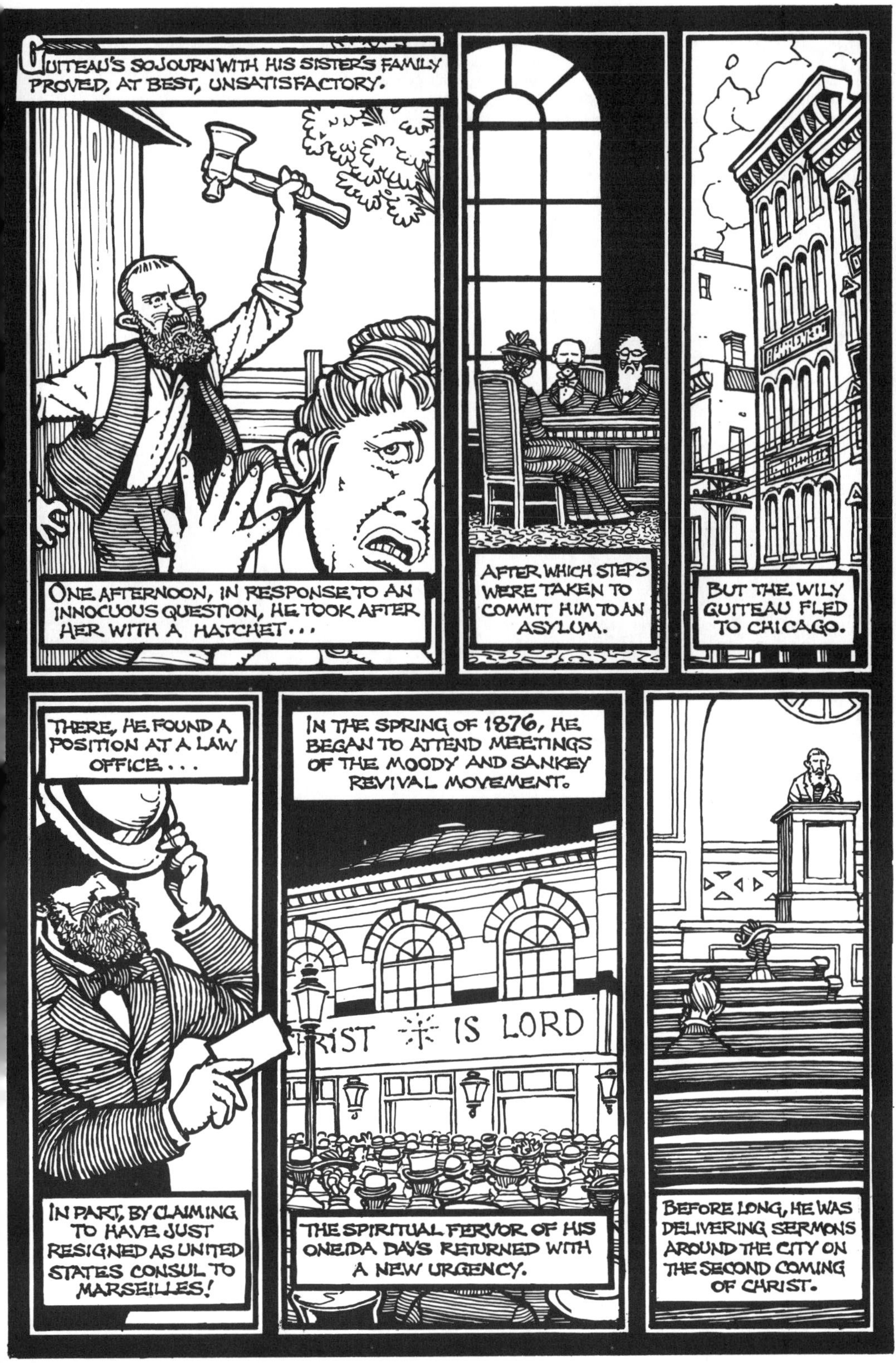
GUITEAU'S SOJOURN WITH HIS SISTER'S FAMILY PROVED, AT BEST, UNSATISFACTORY.
ONE AFTERNOON, IN RESPONSE TO AN INNOCUOUS QUESTION, HE TOOK AFTER HER WITH A HATCHET...
AFTER WHICH STEPS WERE TAKEN TO COMMIT HIM TO AN ASYLUM.
BUT THE WILY GUITEAU FLED TO CHICAGO.
THERE, HE FOUND A POSITION AT A LAW OFFICE...
IN PART, BY CLAIMING TO HAVE JUST RESIGNED AS UNITED STATES CONSUL TO MARSEILLES!
IN THE SPRING OF 1876, HE BEGAN TO ATTEND MEETINGS OF THE MOODY AND SANKEY REVIVAL MOVEMENT.
CHRIST IS LORD
THE SPIRITUAL FERVOR OF HIS ONEIDA DAYS RETURNED WITH A NEW URGENCY.
BEFORE LONG, HE WAS DELIVERING SERMONS AROUND THE CITY ON THE SECOND COMING OF CHRIST.

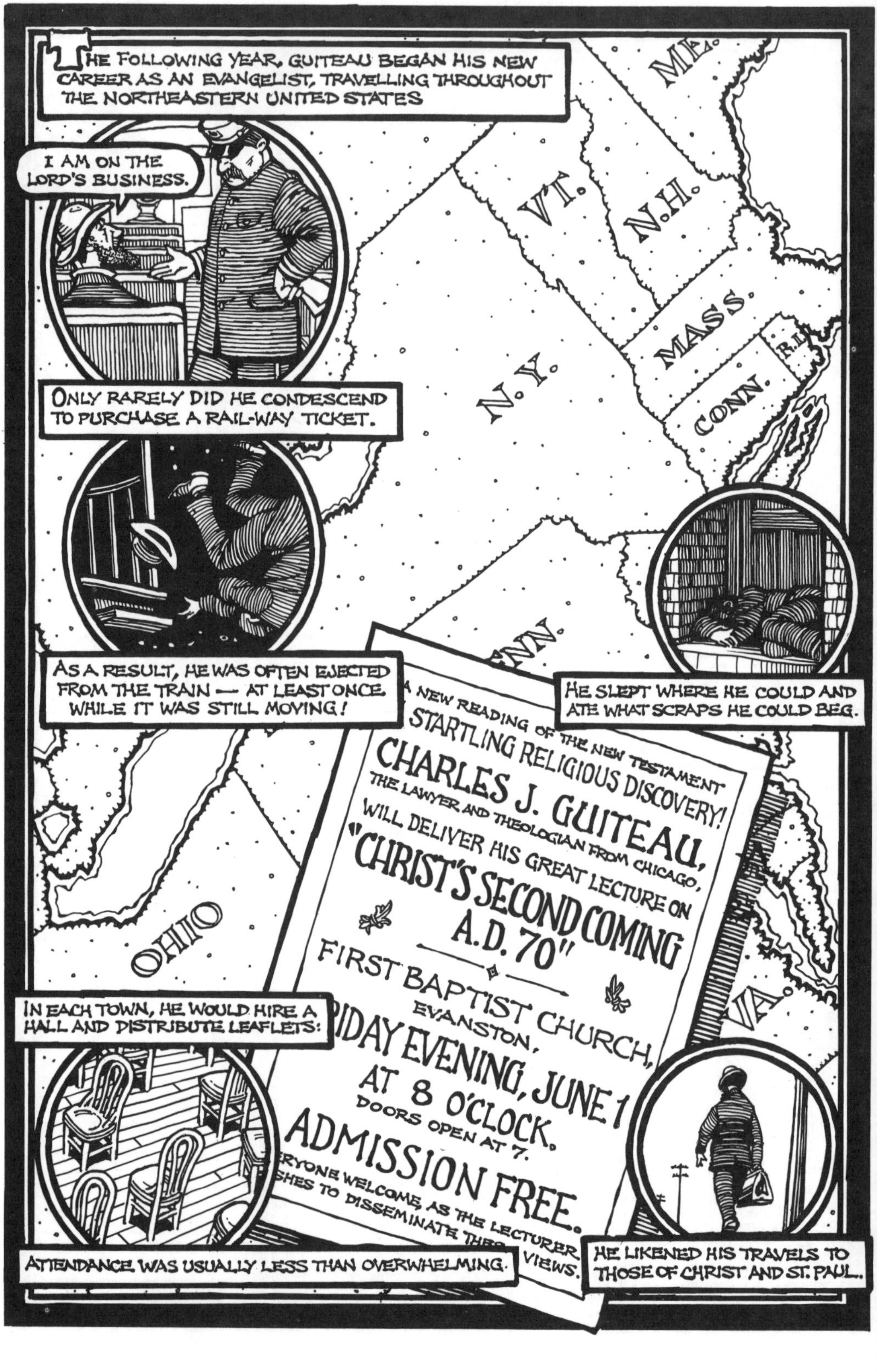

THE FOLLOWING YEAR, GUITEAU BEGAN HIS NEW CAREER AS AN EVANGELIST, TRAVELLING THROUGHOUT THE NORTHEASTERN UNITED STATES
I AM ON THE LORD'S BUSINESS.
ONLY RARELY DID HE CONDESCEND TO PURCHASE A RAIL-WAY TICKET.
AS A RESULT, HE WAS OFTEN EJECTED FROM THE TRAIN — AT LEAST ONCE WHILE IT WAS STILL MOVING!
HE SLEPT WHERE HE COULD AND ATE WHAT SCRAPS HE COULD BEG.
ME.
VT.
N.H.
MASS.
R.I.
CONN.
N.Y.
OHIO
A NEW READING OF THE NEW TESTAMENT
STARTLING RELIGIOUS DISCOVERY!
CHARLES J. GUITEAU,
THE LAWYER AND THEOLOGIAN FROM CHICAGO,
WILL DELIVER HIS GREAT LECTURE ON
"CHRIST'S SECOND COMING A.D. 70"
FIRST BAPTIST CHURCH, EVANSTON,
IDAY EVENING, JUNE 1
AT 8 O'CLOCK.
DOORS OPEN AT 7.
ADMISSION FREE.
VIEWS.
IN EACH TOWN, HE WOULD HIRE A HALL AND DISTRIBUTE LEAFLETS:
ATTENDANCE WAS USUALLY LESS THAN OVERWHELMING.
HE LIKENED HIS TRAVELS TO THOSE OF CHRIST AND ST. PAUL.

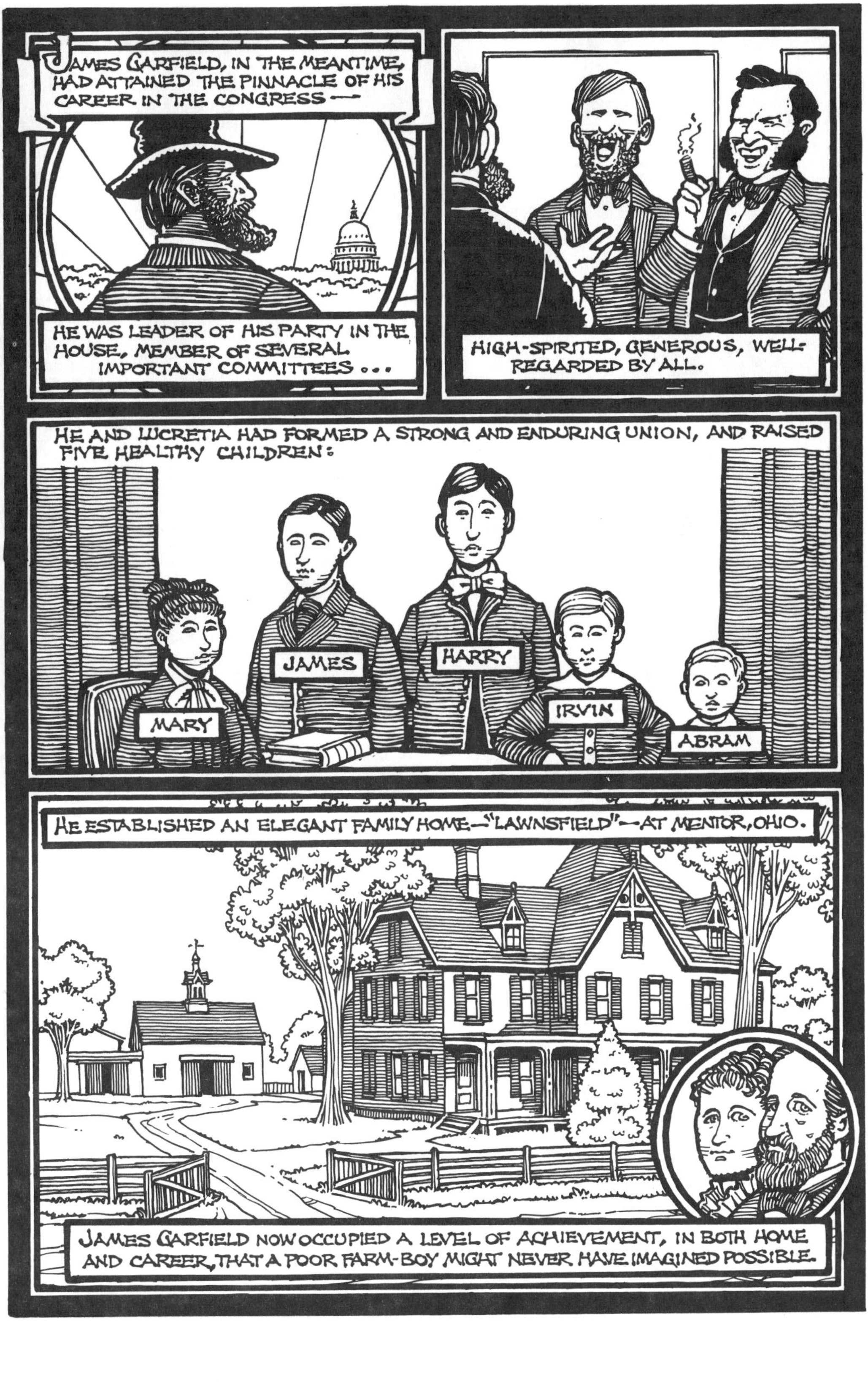
JAMES GARFIELD, IN THE MEANTIME, HAD ATTAINED THE PINNACLE OF HIS CAREER IN THE CONGRESS —
HE WAS LEADER OF HIS PARTY IN THE HOUSE, MEMBER OF SEVERAL IMPORTANT COMMITTEES . . .
HIGH-SPIRITED, GENEROUS, WELL-REGARDED BY ALL.
HE AND LUCRETIA HAD FORMED A STRONG AND ENDURING UNION, AND RAISED FIVE HEALTHY CHILDREN:
MARY
JAMES
HARRY
IRVIN
ABRAM
HE ESTABLISHED AN ELEGANT FAMILY HOME—"LAWNSFIELD"—AT MENTOR, OHIO.
JAMES GARFIELD NOW OCCUPIED A LEVEL OF ACHIEVEMENT, IN BOTH HOME AND CAREER, THAT A POOR FARM-BOY MIGHT NEVER HAVE IMAGINED POSSIBLE.

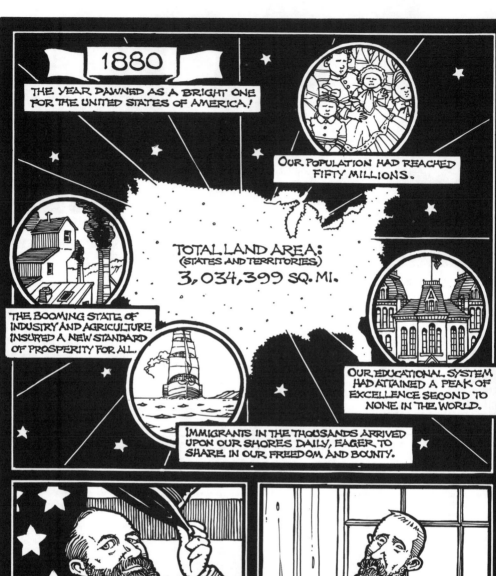

1880

THE YEAR DAWNED AS A BRIGHT ONE FOR THE UNITED STATES OF AMERICA!

OUR POPULATION HAD REACHED FIFTY MILLIONS.

TOTAL LAND AREA:
(STATES AND TERRITORIES)
3,034,399 SQ. MI.

THE BOOMING STATE OF INDUSTRY AND AGRICULTURE INSURED A NEW STANDARD OF PROSPERITY FOR ALL.

OUR EDUCATIONAL SYSTEM HAD ATTAINED A PEAK OF EXCELLENCE SECOND TO NONE IN THE WORLD.

IMMIGRANTS IN THE THOUSANDS ARRIVED UPON OUR SHORES DAILY, EAGER TO SHARE IN OUR FREEDOM AND BOUNTY.

FOR JAMES GARFIELD, THE YEAR BEGAN AUSPICIOUSLY*: IN JANUARY, HE WAS ELECTED BY THE OHIO LEGISLATURE TO THE UNITED STATES SENATE.

FOR CHARLES GUITEAU, GROWN WEARY AFTER THREE YEARS OF EVANGELISM, THE YEAR HELD PROMISE OF A NEW DIRECTION IN LIFE.

PART II.

A DEADLY CAMPAIGN.

IN WHICH THE PREDATOR STALKS AND KILLS ITS PREY.

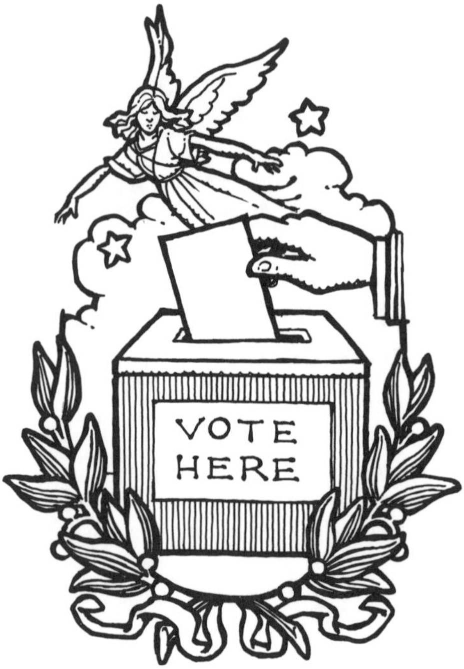
VOTE
HERE

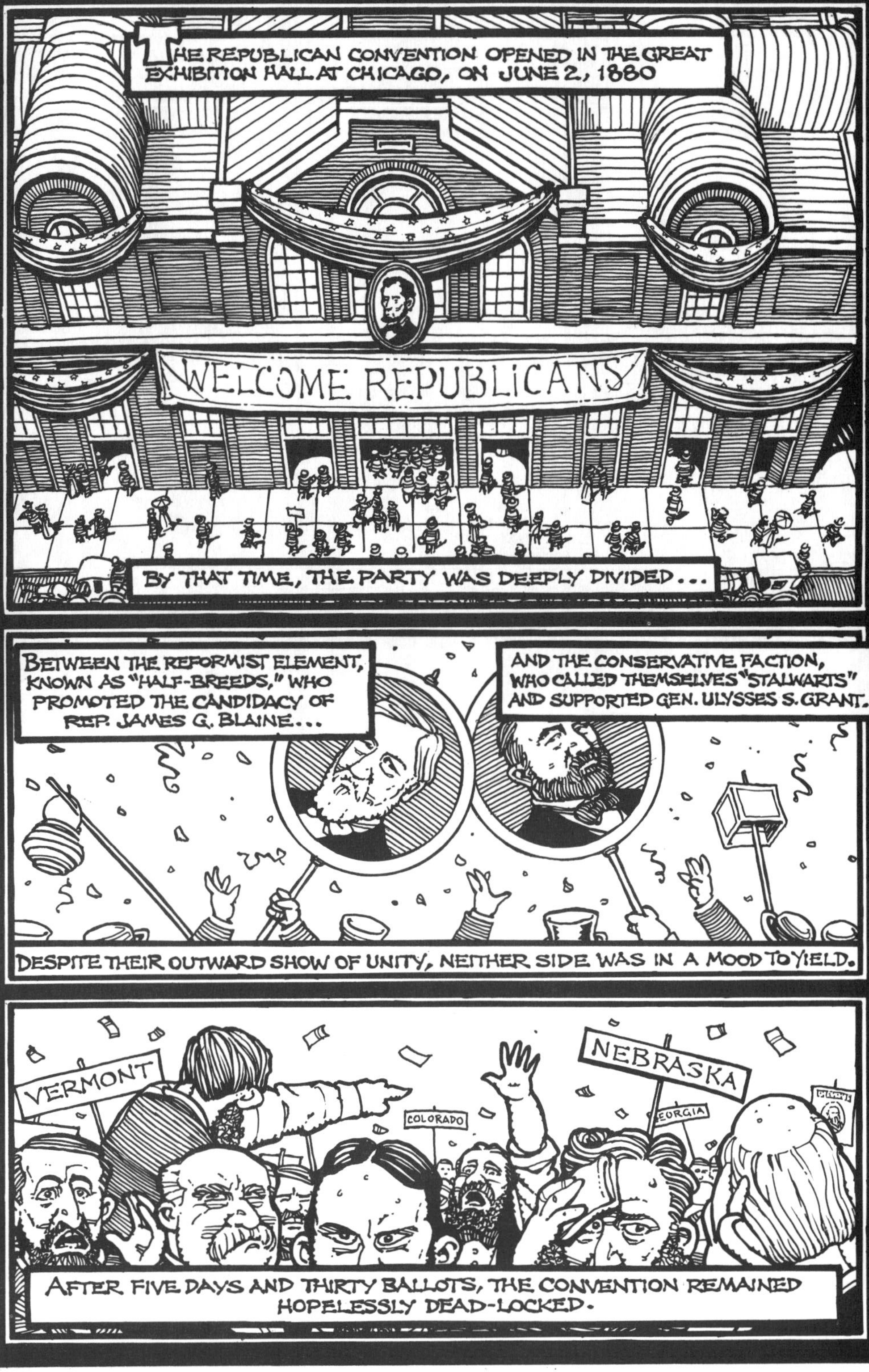
THE REPUBLICAN CONVENTION OPENED IN THE GREAT EXHIBITION HALL AT CHICAGO, ON JUNE 2, 1880
WELCOME REPUBLICANS
BY THAT TIME, THE PARTY WAS DEEPLY DIVIDED...
BETWEEN THE REFORMIST ELEMENT, KNOWN AS "HALF-BREEDS," WHO PROMOTED THE CANDIDACY OF REP. JAMES G. BLAINE...
AND THE CONSERVATIVE FACTION, WHO CALLED THEMSELVES "STALWARTS" AND SUPPORTED GEN. ULYSSES S. GRANT.
DESPITE THEIR OUTWARD SHOW OF UNITY, NEITHER SIDE WAS IN A MOOD TO YIELD.
VERMONT
NEBRASKA
COLORADO
AFTER FIVE DAYS AND THIRTY BALLOTS, THE CONVENTION REMAINED HOPELESSLY DEAD-LOCKED.

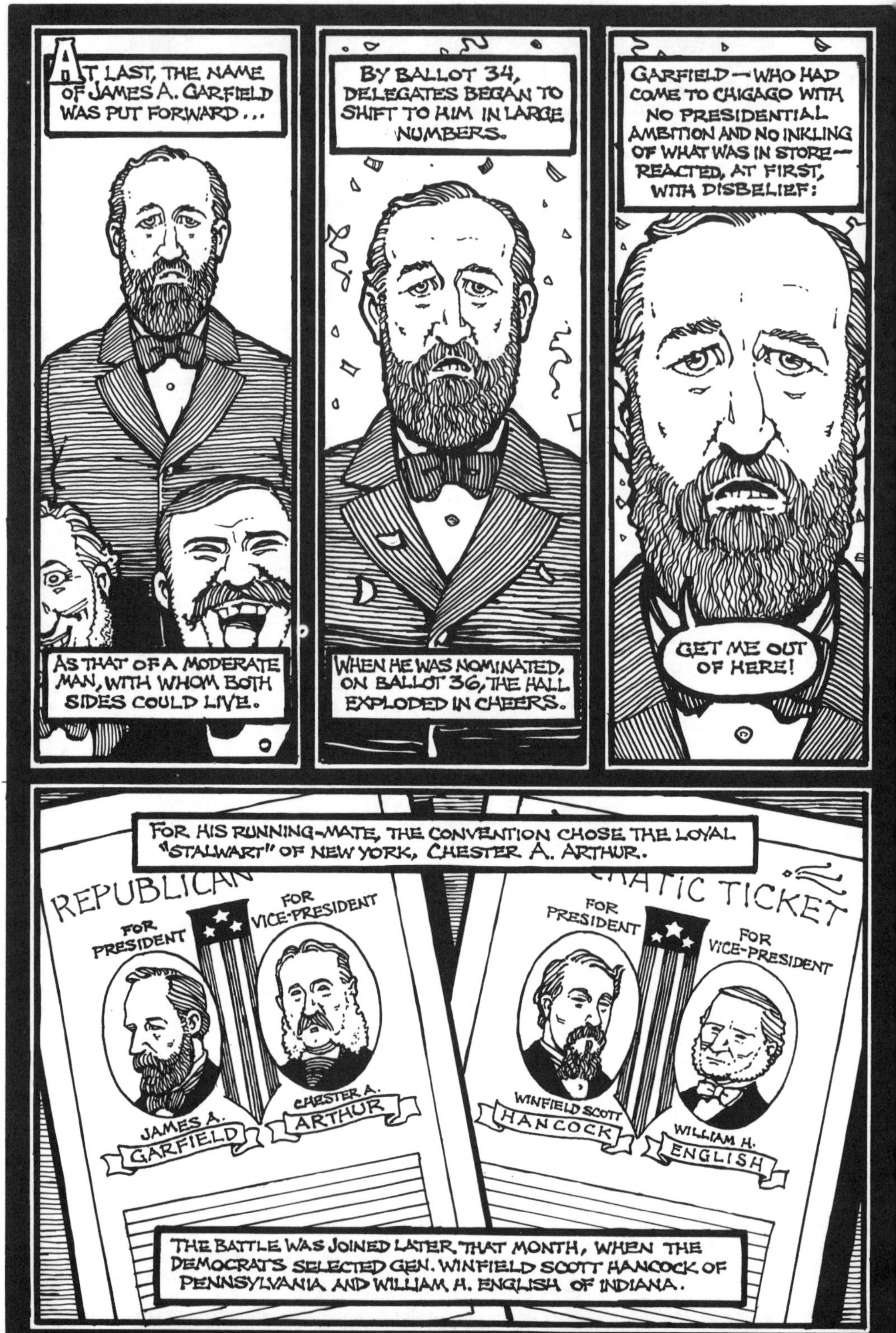
AT LAST, THE NAME OF JAMES A. GARFIELD WAS PUT FORWARD...
AS THAT OF A MODERATE MAN, WITH WHOM BOTH SIDES COULD LIVE.
BY BALLOT 34, DELEGATES BEGAN TO SHIFT TO HIM IN LARGE NUMBERS.
WHEN HE WAS NOMINATED, ON BALLOT 36, THE HALL EXPLODED IN CHEERS.
GARFIELD — WHO HAD COME TO CHICAGO WITH NO PRESIDENTIAL AMBITION AND NO INKLING OF WHAT WAS IN STORE — REACTED, AT FIRST, WITH DISBELIEF:
GET ME OUT OF HERE!
FOR HIS RUNNING-MATE, THE CONVENTION CHOSE THE LOYAL "STALWART" OF NEW YORK, CHESTER A. ARTHUR.
REPUBLICAN
FOR PRESIDENT
FOR VICE-PRESIDENT
JAMES A. GARFIELD
CHESTER A. ARTHUR
CRATIC TICKET
FOR PRESIDENT
FOR VICE-PRESIDENT
WINFIELD SCOTT HANCOCK
WILLIAM H. ENGLISH
THE BATTLE WAS JOINED LATER THAT MONTH, WHEN THE DEMOCRATS SELECTED GEN. WINFIELD SCOTT HANCOCK OF PENNSYLVANIA AND WILLIAM H. ENGLISH OF INDIANA.

IN BOSTON, MEANWHILE, CHARLES GUITEAU, HIMSELF A LOYAL "STALWART," FOLLOWED THE CONVENTION WITH GREAT INTEREST.

HAVING ABANDONED THE PULPIT, HE NOW SOLD POLICIES FOR AN INSURANCE COMPANY.

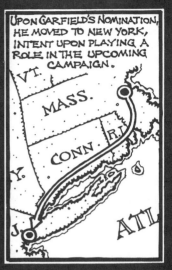

UPON GARFIELD'S NOMINATION, HE MOVED TO NEW YORK, INTENT UPON PLAYING A ROLE IN THE UPCOMING CAMPAIGN.

BY DAY, HE ENCAMPED AT THE REPUBLICAN HEADQUARTERS, INTRODUCING HIMSELF AS A PARTY OFFICIAL . . .

BUT WAS GENERALLY REGARDED AS A NUISANCE AND DISTRACTION.

BY NIGHT, HE WROTE FURIOUSLY.

GARFIELD AGAINST HANCOCK

CHAS. J. GUITEAU

A SPEECH HE HAD COMPOSED FOR GEN. GRANT WAS REVISED INTO ONE IN RINGING SUPPORT OF GARFIELD.

IT WAS A SPEECH THAT HE KNEW WOULD SWEEP THE PARTY TO VICTORY.

AUGUST 6 SAW A MASSIVE REPUBLICAN RALLY AT THE FIFTH AVENUE HOTEL.

ALL THE LUMINARIES OF THE PARTY WERE IN ATTENDANCE, IN THE CONTINUING EFFORT TO MEND THE DIFFERENCES BETWEEN THEIR OPPOSING FACTIONS.

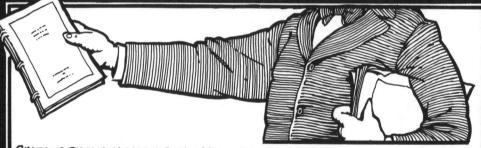

CHARLES GUITEAU WOVE HIS WAY AMONGST THE CROWD, SHAKING HANDS AND PASSING OUT COPIES OF HIS SPEECH.

HE CAUGHT ONLY A GLIMPSE OF GARFIELD BUT SENT A COPY TO THE CANDIDATE'S SUITE.

NO PERSON THERE COULD HAVE BEEN PLEASED TO SEE THIS NERVOUS, VOLUBLE LITTLE MAN COMING THEIR WAY.

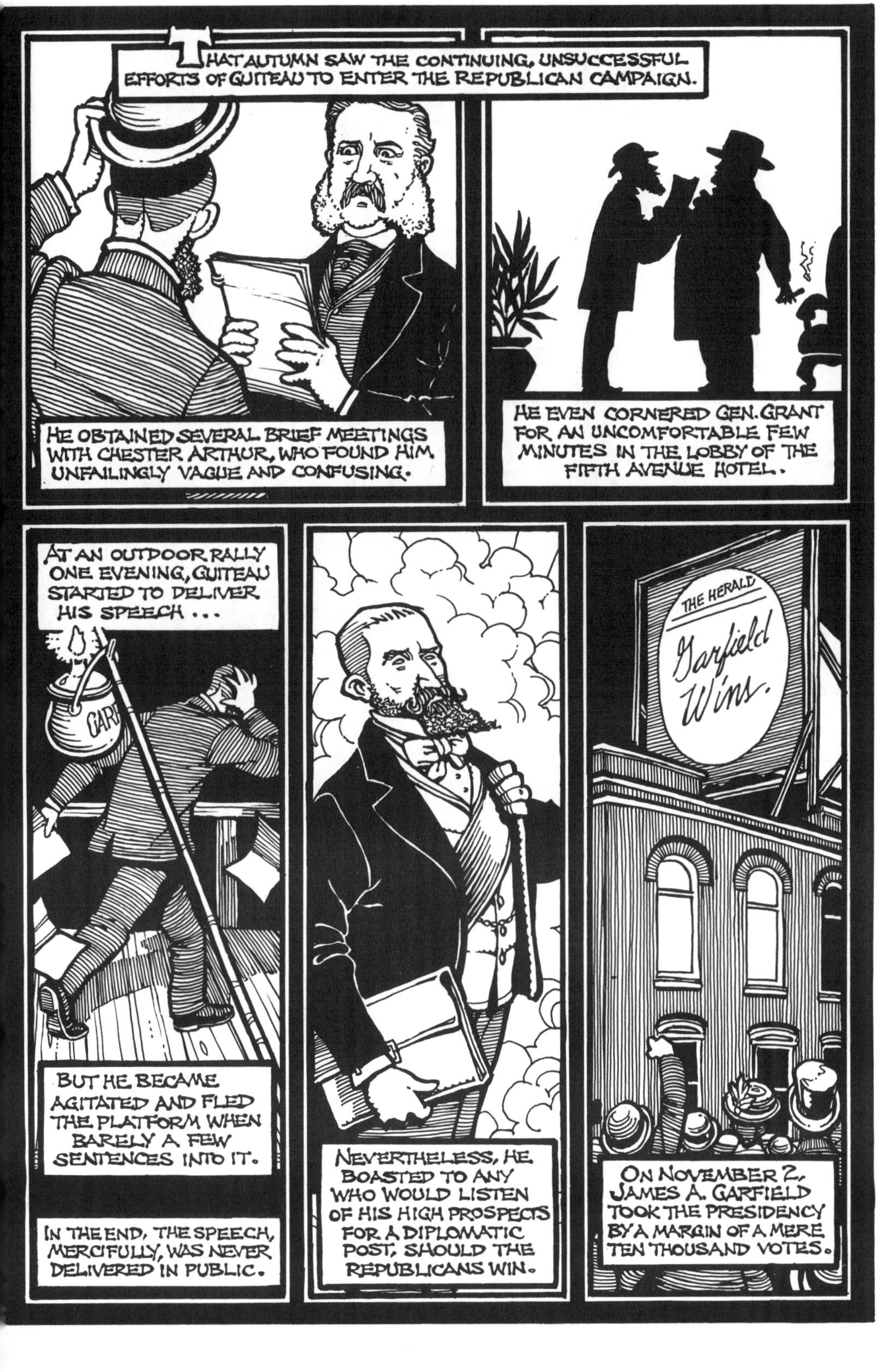
THAT AUTUMN SAW THE CONTINUING, UNSUCCESSFUL EFFORTS OF GUITEAU TO ENTER THE REPUBLICAN CAMPAIGN.
HE OBTAINED SEVERAL BRIEF MEETINGS WITH CHESTER ARTHUR, WHO FOUND HIM UNFAILINGLY VAGUE AND CONFUSING.
HE EVEN CORNERED GEN. GRANT FOR AN UNCOMFORTABLE FEW MINUTES IN THE LOBBY OF THE FIFTH AVENUE HOTEL.
AT AN OUTDOOR RALLY ONE EVENING, GUITEAU STARTED TO DELIVER HIS SPEECH ...
GARF
BUT HE BECAME AGITATED AND FLED THE PLATFORM WHEN BARELY A FEW SENTENCES INTO IT.
IN THE END, THE SPEECH, MERCIFULLY, WAS NEVER DELIVERED IN PUBLIC.
NEVERTHELESS, HE BOASTED TO ANY WHO WOULD LISTEN OF HIS HIGH PROSPECTS FOR A DIPLOMATIC POST, SHOULD THE REPUBLICANS WIN.
THE HERALD
Garfield Wins.
ON NOVEMBER 2, JAMES A. GARFIELD TOOK THE PRESIDENCY BY A MARGIN OF A MERE TEN THOUSAND VOTES.

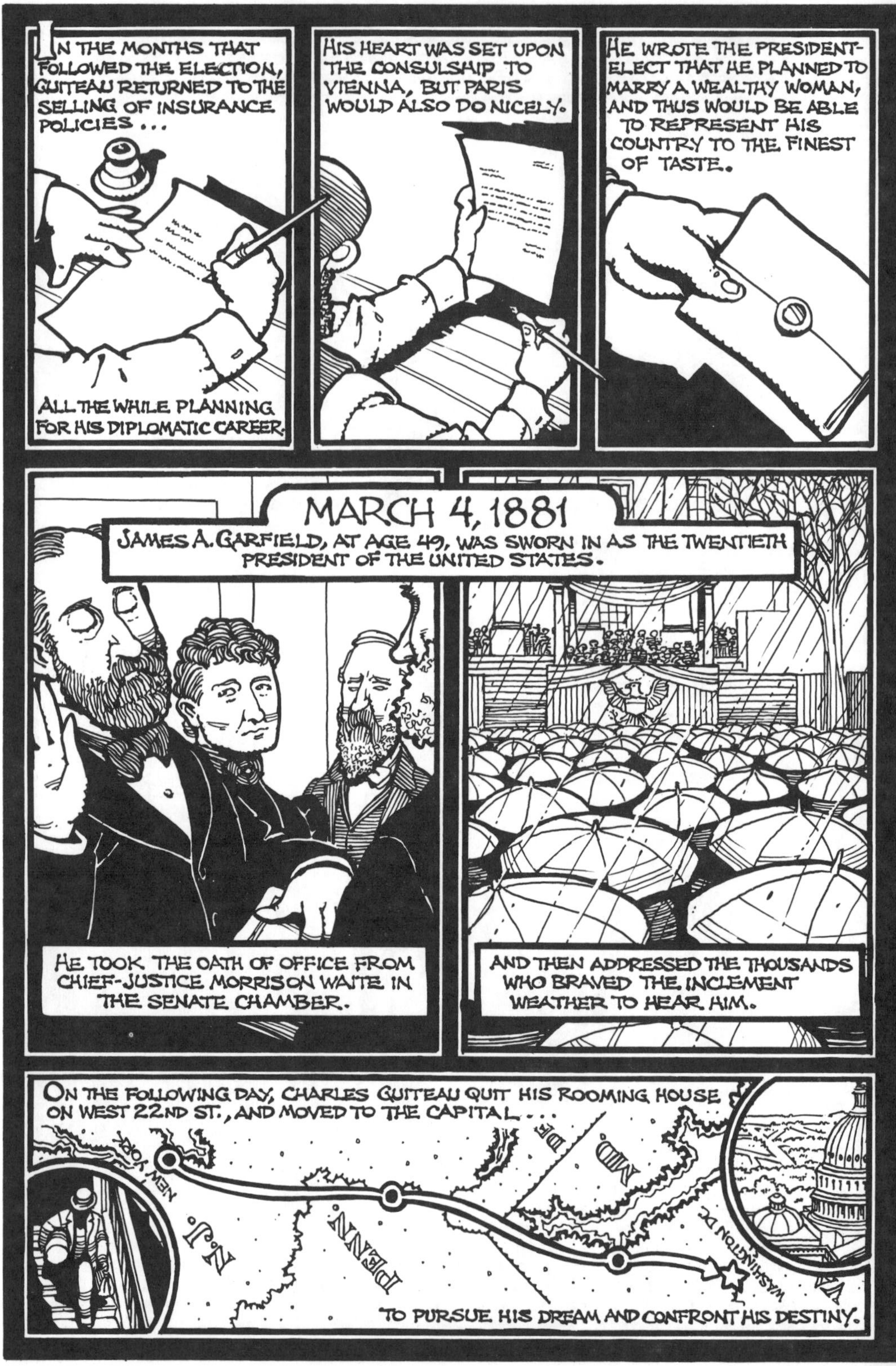
IN THE MONTHS THAT FOLLOWED THE ELECTION, GUITEAU RETURNED TO THE SELLING OF INSURANCE POLICIES . . .
ALL THE WHILE PLANNING FOR HIS DIPLOMATIC CAREER.
HIS HEART WAS SET UPON THE CONSULSHIP TO VIENNA, BUT PARIS WOULD ALSO DO NICELY.
HE WROTE THE PRESIDENT-ELECT THAT HE PLANNED TO MARRY A WEALTHY WOMAN, AND THUS WOULD BE ABLE TO REPRESENT HIS COUNTRY TO THE FINEST OF TASTE.
MARCH 4, 1881
JAMES A. GARFIELD, AT AGE 49, WAS SWORN IN AS THE TWENTIETH PRESIDENT OF THE UNITED STATES.
HE TOOK THE OATH OF OFFICE FROM CHIEF-JUSTICE MORRISON WAITE IN THE SENATE CHAMBER.
AND THEN ADDRESSED THE THOUSANDS WHO BRAVED THE INCLEMENT WEATHER TO HEAR HIM.
ON THE FOLLOWING DAY, CHARLES GUITEAU QUIT HIS ROOMING HOUSE ON WEST 22ND ST., AND MOVED TO THE CAPITAL . . .
NEW YORK
N.J.
PENN
DE
MD
WASHINGTON DC
VA
TO PURSUE HIS DREAM AND CONFRONT HIS DESTINY.

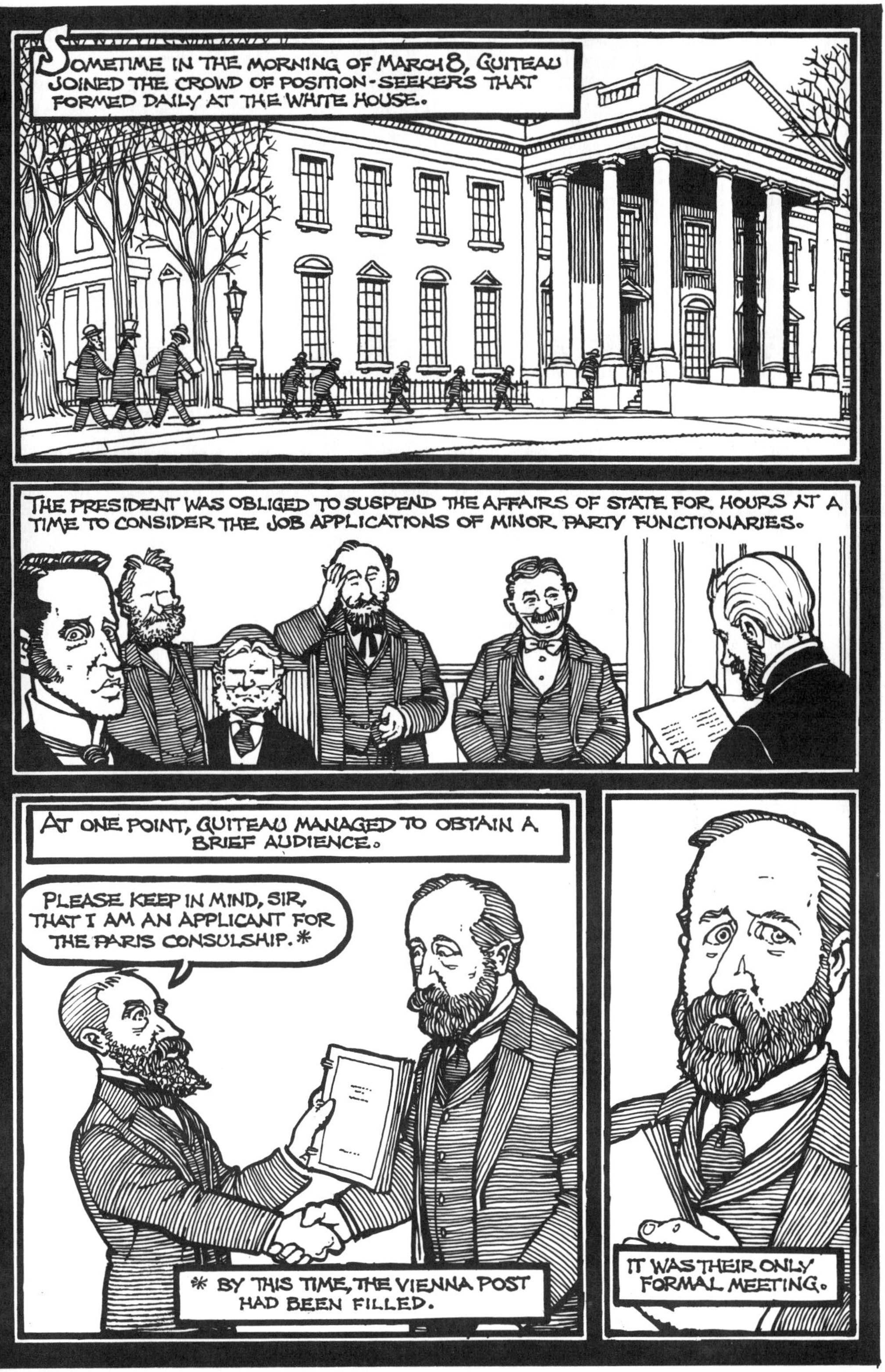
SOMETIME IN THE MORNING OF MARCH 8, GUITEAU JOINED THE CROWD OF POSITION-SEEKERS THAT FORMED DAILY AT THE WHITE HOUSE.
THE PRESIDENT WAS OBLIGED TO SUSPEND THE AFFAIRS OF STATE FOR HOURS AT A TIME TO CONSIDER THE JOB APPLICATIONS OF MINOR PARTY FUNCTIONARIES.
AT ONE POINT, GUITEAU MANAGED TO OBTAIN A BRIEF AUDIENCE.
PLEASE KEEP IN MIND, SIR, THAT I AM AN APPLICANT FOR THE PARIS CONSULSHIP.*
* BY THIS TIME, THE VIENNA POST HAD BEEN FILLED.
IT WAS THEIR ONLY FORMAL MEETING.

GUITEAU ALSO PRESSED HIS CASE TO JAMES G. BLAINE, WHO HAD BEEN APPOINTED SECRETARY OF STATE.

IF YOU CAN SEE YOUR WAY, SIR, TO EXPEDITE MY APPLICATION...

HE WROTE LETTERS AND MEMORANDA DAILY: TO THE PRESS, TO SELECTED MEMBERS OF CONGRESS, TO THE SECRETARY OF STATE, AND OF COURSE TO THE PRESIDENT:

MR. PRESIDENT,
I PRESUME, MY APPOINTMENT WILL BE PROMPTLY CONFIRMED. THERE IS NOTHING AGAINST ME. I CLAIM TO BE A GENTLEMAN AND A CHRISTIAN.
CHARLES J. GUITEAU

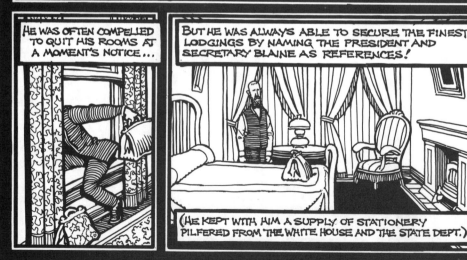

HE WAS OFTEN COMPELLED TO QUIT HIS ROOMS AT A MOMENT'S NOTICE...

BUT HE WAS ALWAYS ABLE TO SECURE THE FINEST LODGINGS BY NAMING THE PRESIDENT AND SECRETARY BLAINE AS REFERENCES!

(HE KEPT WITH HIM A SUPPLY OF STATIONERY PILFERED FROM THE WHITE HOUSE AND THE STATE DEPT.)

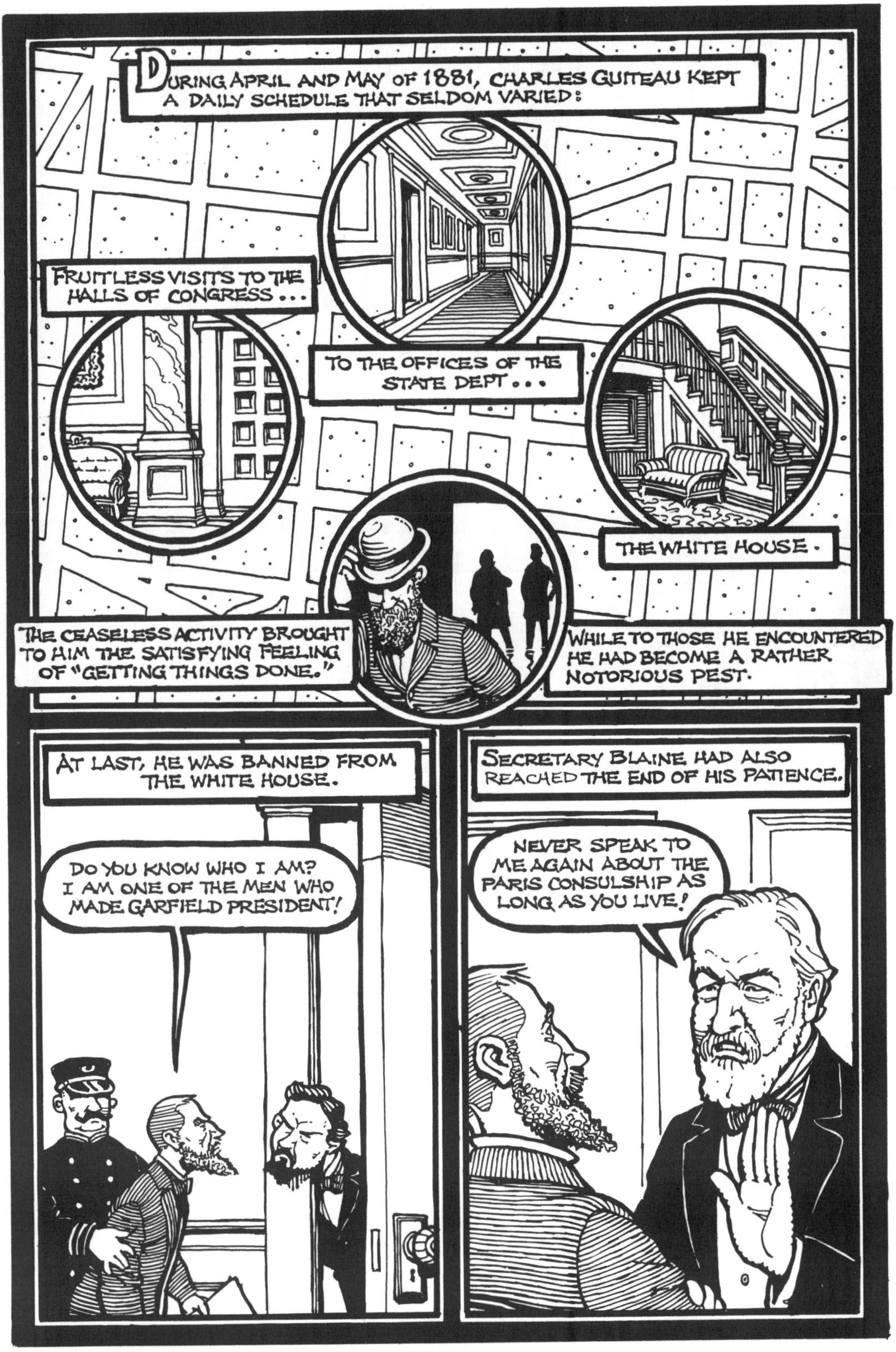
During April and May of 1881, Charles Guiteau kept a daily schedule that seldom varied:
Fruitless visits to the halls of Congress...
To the offices of the State Dept...
The White House.
The ceaseless activity brought to him the satisfying feeling of "getting things done."
While to those he encountered he had become a rather notorious pest.
At last, he was banned from the White House.
Do you know who I am? I am one of the men who made Garfield president!
Secretary Blaine had also reached the end of his patience.
Never speak to me again about the Paris consulship as long as you live!

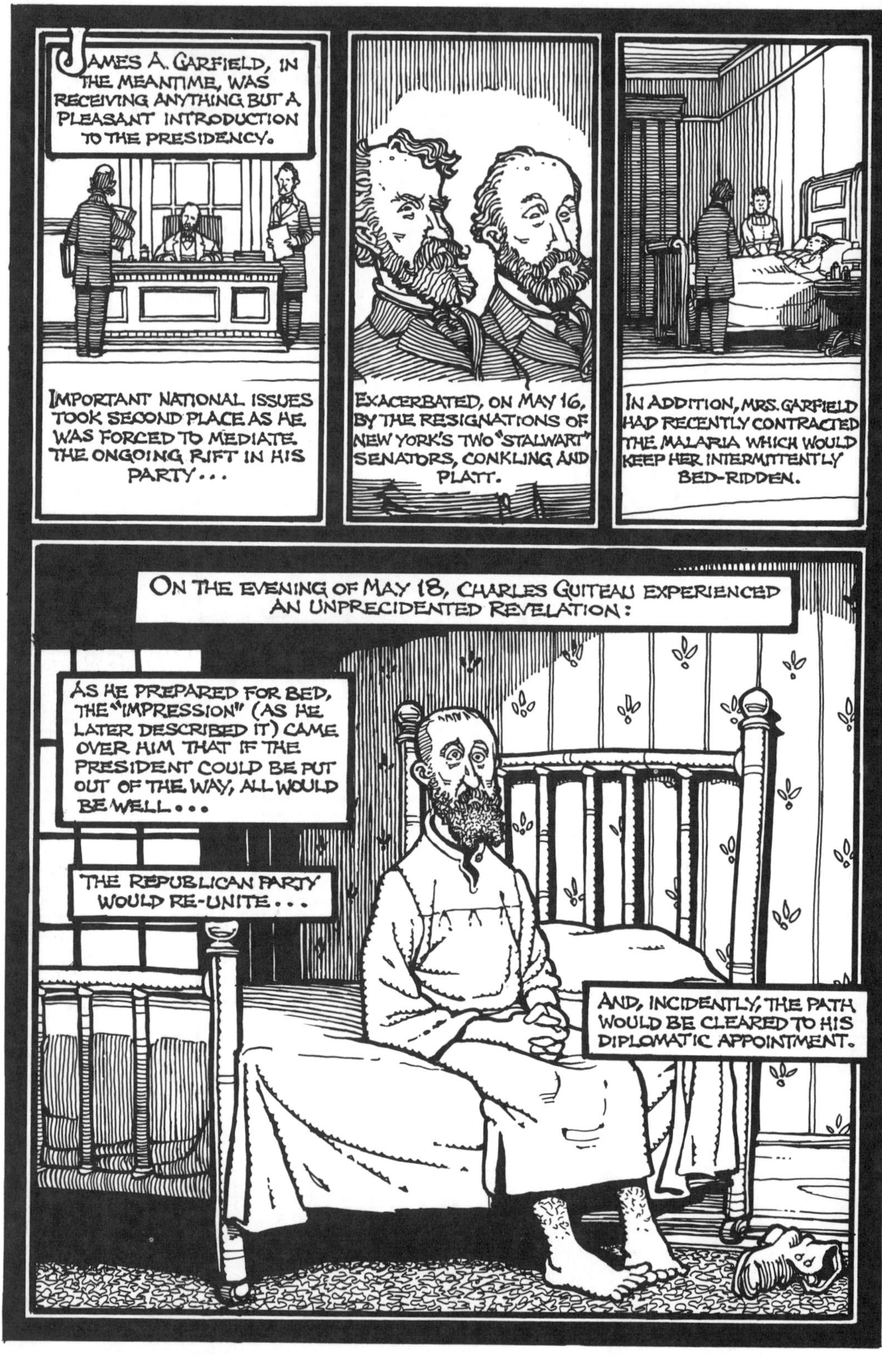
JAMES A. GARFIELD, IN THE MEANTIME, WAS RECEIVING ANYTHING BUT A PLEASANT INTRODUCTION TO THE PRESIDENCY.
IMPORTANT NATIONAL ISSUES TOOK SECOND PLACE AS HE WAS FORCED TO MEDIATE THE ONGOING RIFT IN HIS PARTY...
EXACERBATED, ON MAY 16, BY THE RESIGNATIONS OF NEW YORK'S TWO "STALWART" SENATORS, CONKLING AND PLATT.
IN ADDITION, MRS. GARFIELD HAD RECENTLY CONTRACTED THE MALARIA WHICH WOULD KEEP HER INTERMITTENTLY BED-RIDDEN.
ON THE EVENING OF MAY 18, CHARLES GUITEAU EXPERIENCED AN UNPRECIDENTED REVELATION:
AS HE PREPARED FOR BED, THE "IMPRESSION" (AS HE LATER DESCRIBED IT) CAME OVER HIM THAT IF THE PRESIDENT COULD BE PUT OUT OF THE WAY, ALL WOULD BE WELL...
THE REPUBLICAN PARTY WOULD RE-UNITE...
AND, INCIDENTLY, THE PATH WOULD BE CLEARED TO HIS DIPLOMATIC APPOINTMENT.

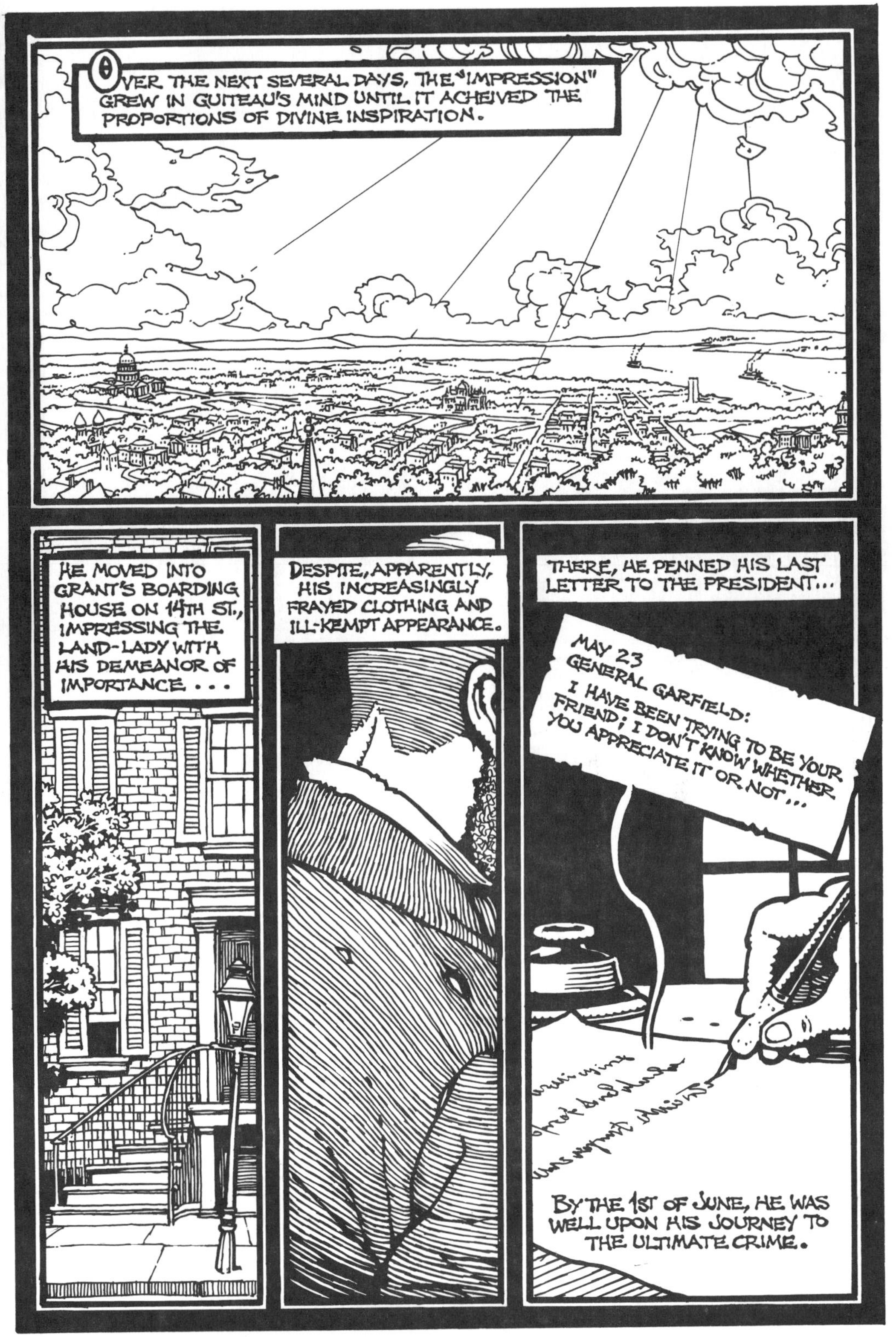
OVER THE NEXT SEVERAL DAYS, THE "IMPRESSION" GREW IN GUITEAU'S MIND UNTIL IT ACHEIVED THE PROPORTIONS OF DIVINE INSPIRATION.
HE MOVED INTO GRANT'S BOARDING HOUSE ON 14TH ST., IMPRESSING THE LAND-LADY WITH HIS DEMEANOR OF IMPORTANCE . . .
DESPITE, APPARENTLY, HIS INCREASINGLY FRAYED CLOTHING AND ILL-KEMPT APPEARANCE.
THERE, HE PENNED HIS LAST LETTER TO THE PRESIDENT...
MAY 23
GENERAL GARFIELD:
I HAVE BEEN TRYING TO BE YOUR FRIEND; I DON'T KNOW WHETHER YOU APPRECIATE IT OR NOT...
BY THE 1ST OF JUNE, HE WAS WELL UPON HIS JOURNEY TO THE ULTIMATE CRIME.

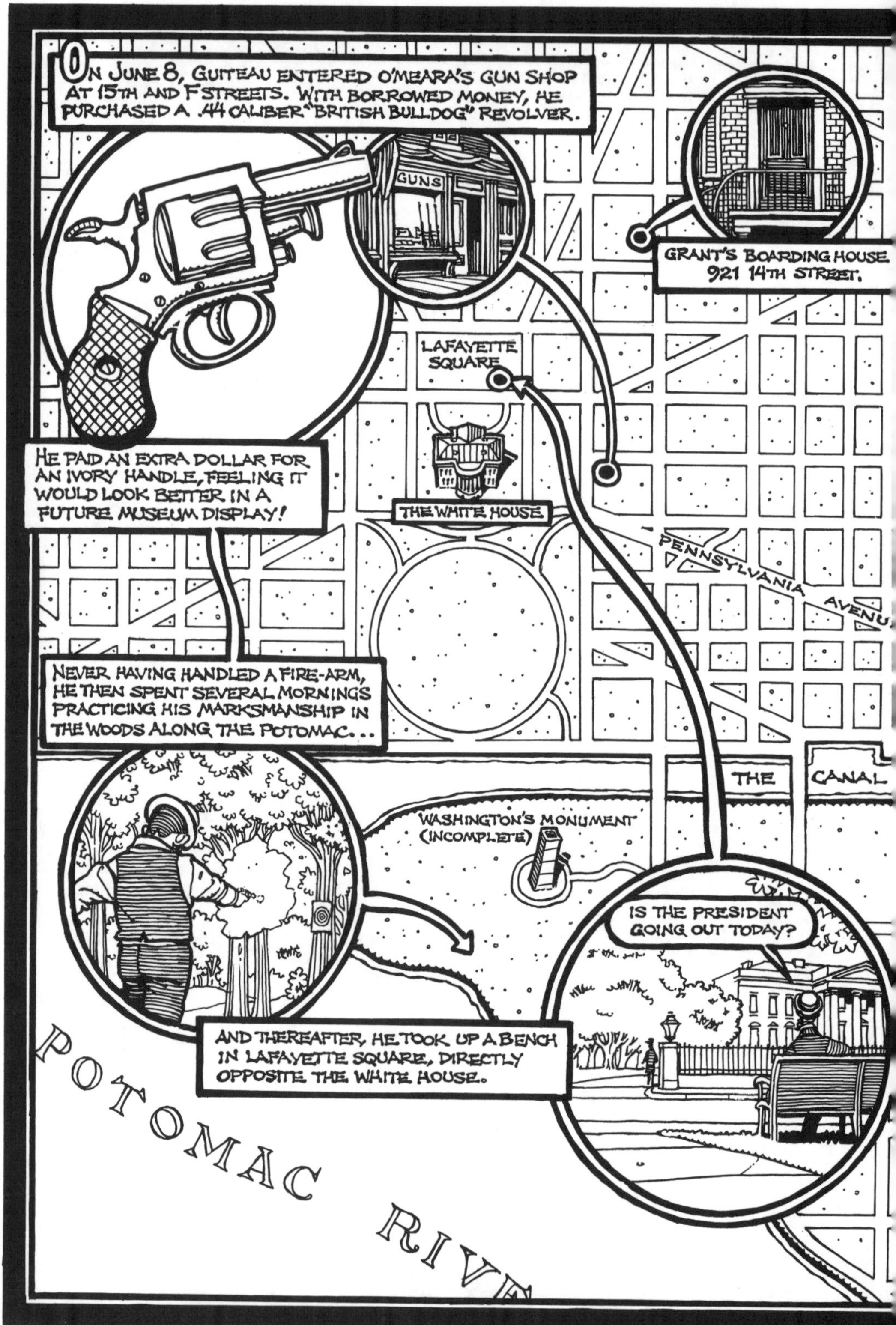

On June 8, Guiteau entered O'Meara's gun shop at 15th and F streets. With borrowed money, he purchased a .44 caliber "British Bulldog" revolver.
GUNS
Grant's Boarding House 921 14th Street.
Lafayette Square
He paid an extra dollar for an ivory handle, feeling it would look better in a future museum display!
The White House
Pennsylvania Avenu
Never having handled a fire-arm, he then spent several mornings practicing his marksmanship in the woods along the Potomac...
The Canal
Washington's Monument (incomplete)
Is the President going out today?
And thereafter, he took up a bench in Lafayette Square, directly opposite the White House.
Potomac Rive

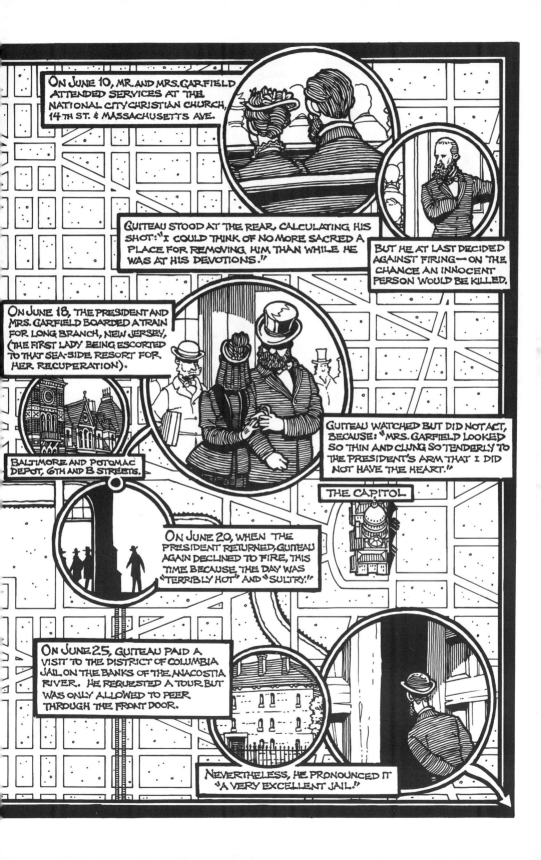

ON JUNE 10, MR. AND MRS. GARFIELD ATTENDED SERVICES AT THE NATIONAL CITY CHRISTIAN CHURCH, 14TH ST. & MASSACHUSETTS AVE.

GUITEAU STOOD AT THE REAR, CALCULATING HIS SHOT: "I COULD THINK OF NO MORE SACRED A PLACE FOR REMOVING HIM THAN WHILE HE WAS AT HIS DEVOTIONS."

BUT HE AT LAST DECIDED AGAINST FIRING — ON THE CHANCE AN INNOCENT PERSON WOULD BE KILLED.

ON JUNE 18, THE PRESIDENT AND MRS. GARFIELD BOARDED A TRAIN FOR LONG BRANCH, NEW JERSEY, (THE FIRST LADY BEING ESCORTED TO THAT SEA-SIDE RESORT FOR HER RECUPERATION).

BALTIMORE AND POTOMAC DEPOT, 6TH AND B STREETS.

GUITEAU WATCHED BUT DID NOT ACT, BECAUSE: "MRS. GARFIELD LOOKED SO THIN AND CLUNG SO TENDERLY TO THE PRESIDENT'S ARM THAT I DID NOT HAVE THE HEART."

THE CAPITOL

ON JUNE 20, WHEN THE PRESIDENT RETURNED, GUITEAU AGAIN DECLINED TO FIRE, THIS TIME BECAUSE THE DAY WAS "TERRIBLY HOT" AND "SULTRY."

ON JUNE 25, GUITEAU PAID A VISIT TO THE DISTRICT OF COLUMBIA JAIL ON THE BANKS OF THE ANACOSTIA RIVER. HE REQUESTED A TOUR BUT WAS ONLY ALLOWED TO PEER THROUGH THE FRONT DOOR.

NEVERTHELESS, HE PRONOUNCED IT "A VERY EXCELLENT JAIL!"

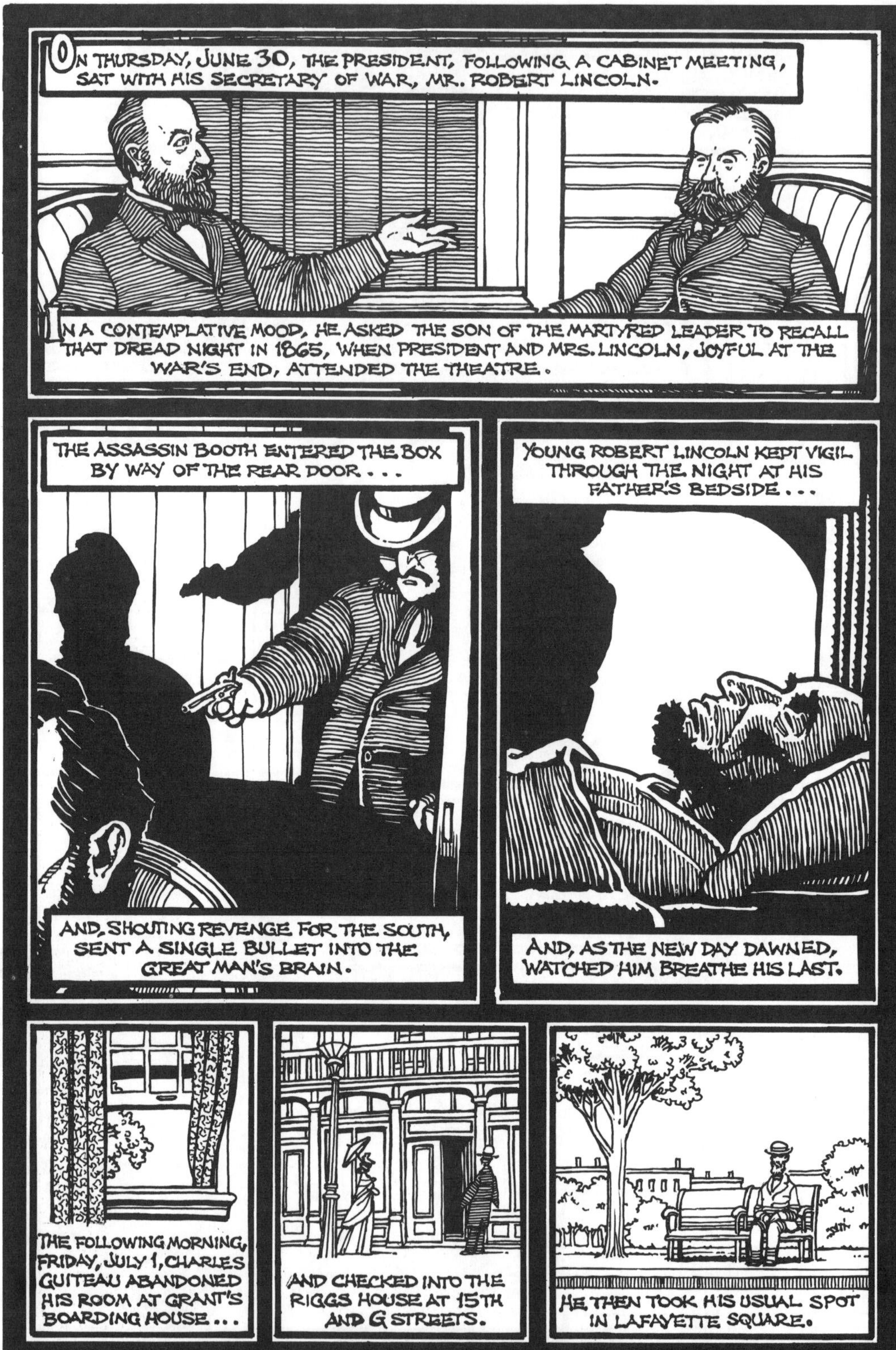
ON THURSDAY, JUNE 30, THE PRESIDENT, FOLLOWING A CABINET MEETING, SAT WITH HIS SECRETARY OF WAR, MR. ROBERT LINCOLN.
IN A CONTEMPLATIVE MOOD, HE ASKED THE SON OF THE MARTYRED LEADER TO RECALL THAT DREAD NIGHT IN 1865, WHEN PRESIDENT AND MRS. LINCOLN, JOYFUL AT THE WAR'S END, ATTENDED THE THEATRE.
THE ASSASSIN BOOTH ENTERED THE BOX BY WAY OF THE REAR DOOR . . .
AND, SHOUTING REVENGE FOR THE SOUTH, SENT A SINGLE BULLET INTO THE GREAT MAN'S BRAIN.
YOUNG ROBERT LINCOLN KEPT VIGIL THROUGH THE NIGHT AT HIS FATHER'S BEDSIDE . . .
AND, AS THE NEW DAY DAWNED, WATCHED HIM BREATHE HIS LAST.
THE FOLLOWING MORNING, FRIDAY, JULY 1, CHARLES GUITEAU ABANDONED HIS ROOM AT GRANT'S BOARDING HOUSE . . .
AND CHECKED INTO THE RIGGS HOUSE AT 15TH AND G STREETS.
HE THEN TOOK HIS USUAL SPOT IN LAFAYETTE SQUARE.

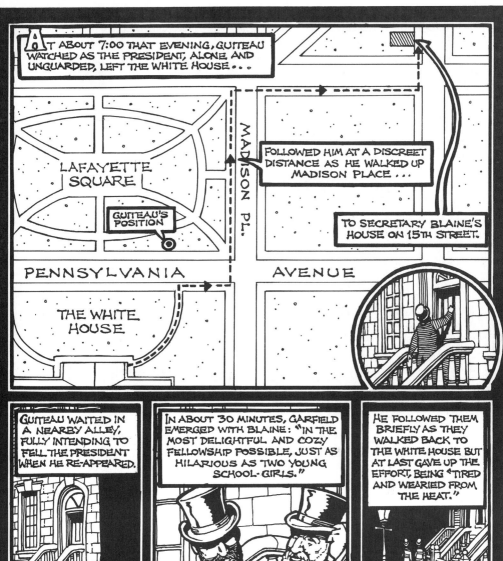

AT ABOUT 7:00 THAT EVENING, GUITEAU WATCHED AS THE PRESIDENT, ALONE AND UNGUARDED, LEFT THE WHITE HOUSE...

LAFAYETTE SQUARE

GUITEAU'S POSITION

MADISON PL.

FOLLOWED HIM AT A DISCREET DISTANCE AS HE WALKED UP MADISON PLACE...

TO SECRETARY BLAINE'S HOUSE ON 15TH STREET.

PENNSYLVANIA   AVENUE

THE WHITE HOUSE

GUITEAU WAITED IN A NEARBY ALLEY, FULLY INTENDING TO FELL THE PRESIDENT WHEN HE RE-APPEARED.

IN ABOUT 30 MINUTES, GARFIELD EMERGED WITH BLAINE: "IN THE MOST DELIGHTFUL AND COZY FELLOWSHIP POSSIBLE, JUST AS HILARIOUS AS TWO YOUNG SCHOOL-GIRLS."

HE FOLLOWED THEM BRIEFLY AS THEY WALKED BACK TO THE WHITE HOUSE BUT AT LAST GAVE UP THE EFFORT, BEING "TIRED AND WEARIED FROM THE HEAT."

SATURDAY JULY 2
THE DAY OF INFAMY

CHARLES GUITEAU AROSE IN ROOM 222 OF THE RIGGS HOUSE, CERTAIN THAT THIS WOULD BE THE DAY.

(THE PRESIDENT, IT HAD BEEN ANNOUNCED, WAS TO LEAVE THAT MORNING FOR A TWO-WEEK HOLIDAY.)

HE DRESSED IN HIS BEST SUIT AND TOOK A LEISURELY STROLL THROUGH LAFAYETTE SQUARE.

INSIDE THE WHITE HOUSE, MEANWHILE, THE PRESIDENT AWOKE IN A CHEERFUL HUMOR...

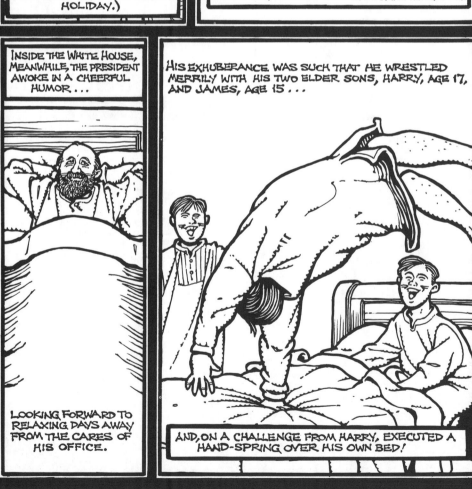

LOOKING FORWARD TO RELAXING DAYS AWAY FROM THE CARES OF HIS OFFICE.

HIS EXHUBERANCE WAS SUCH THAT HE WRESTLED MERRILY WITH HIS TWO ELDER SONS, HARRY, AGE 17, AND JAMES, AGE 15...

AND, ON A CHALLENGE FROM HARRY, EXECUTED A HAND-SPRING OVER HIS OWN BED!

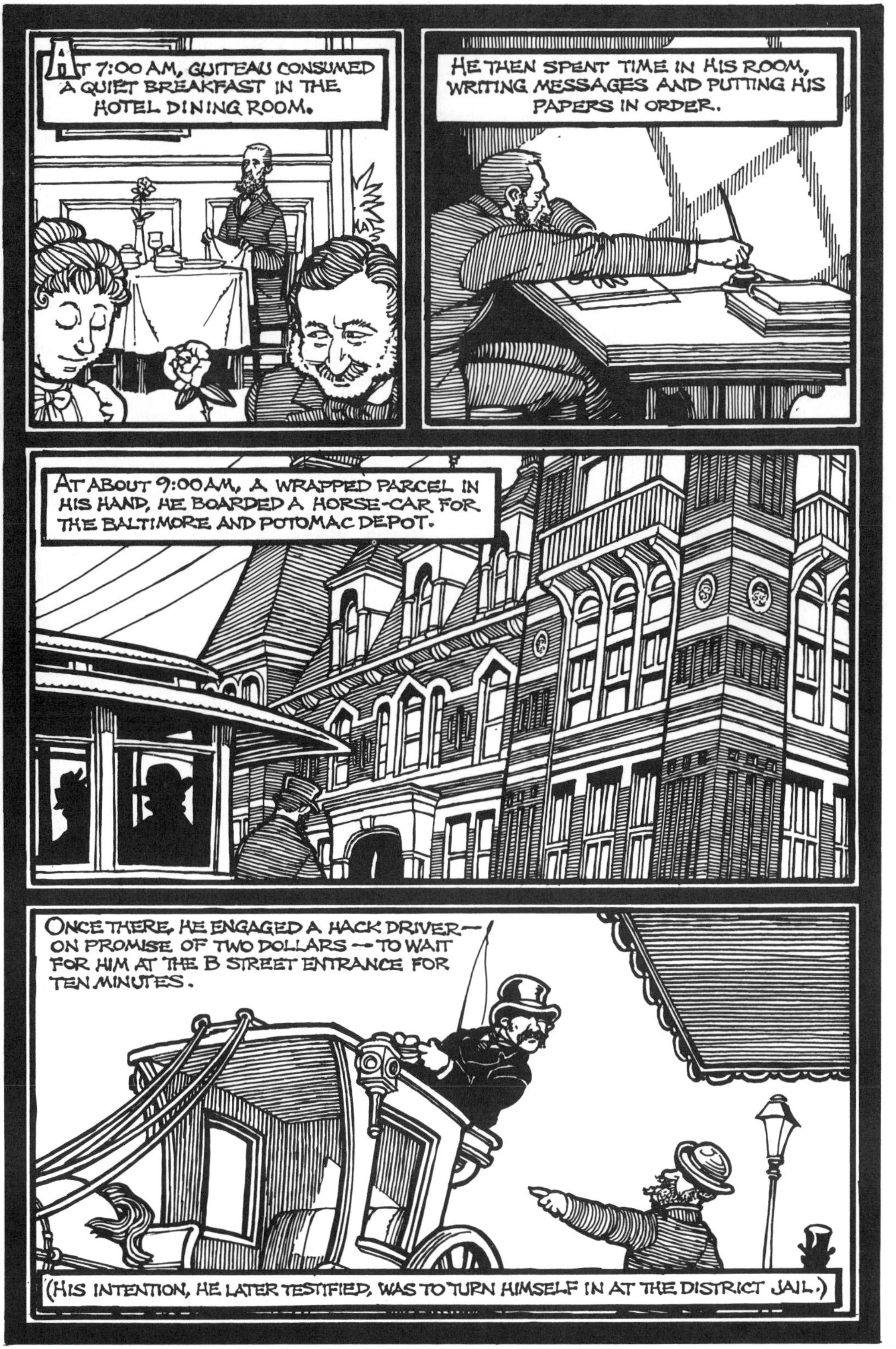
At 7:00 AM, Guiteau consumed a quiet breakfast in the hotel dining room.
He then spent time in his room, writing messages and putting his papers in order.
At about 9:00 AM, a wrapped parcel in his hand, he boarded a horse-car for the Baltimore and Potomac Depot.
Once there, he engaged a hack driver— on promise of two dollars — to wait for him at the B Street entrance for ten minutes.
(His intention, he later testified, was to turn himself in at the District Jail.)

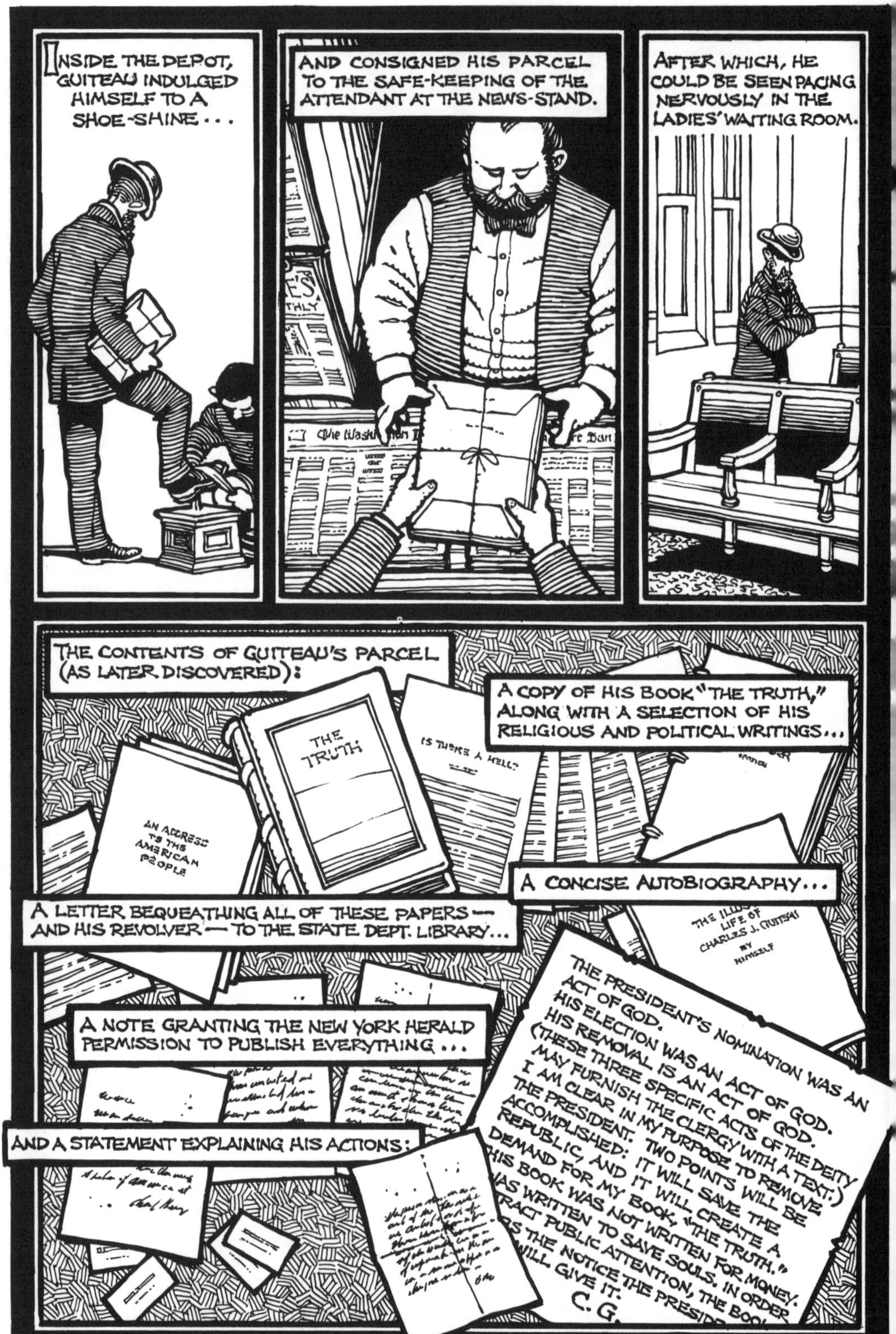
INSIDE THE DEPOT, GUITEAU INDULGED HIMSELF TO A SHOE-SHINE . . .
AND CONSIGNED HIS PARCEL TO THE SAFE-KEEPING OF THE ATTENDANT AT THE NEWS-STAND.
AFTER WHICH, HE COULD BE SEEN PACING NERVOUSLY IN THE LADIES' WAITING ROOM.
THE CONTENTS OF GUITEAU'S PARCEL (AS LATER DISCOVERED):
A COPY OF HIS BOOK "THE TRUTH," ALONG WITH A SELECTION OF HIS RELIGIOUS AND POLITICAL WRITINGS . . .
THE TRUTH
IS THERE A HELL?
AN ADDRESS TO THE AMERICAN PEOPLE
A CONCISE AUTOBIOGRAPHY . . .
A LETTER BEQUEATHING ALL OF THESE PAPERS — AND HIS REVOLVER — TO THE STATE DEPT. LIBRARY . . .
A NOTE GRANTING THE NEW YORK HERALD PERMISSION TO PUBLISH EVERYTHING . . .
AND A STATEMENT EXPLAINING HIS ACTIONS:
THE PRESIDENT'S NOMINATION WAS AN
ACT OF GOD.
HIS ELECTION WAS AN ACT OF GOD.
HIS REMOVAL IS AN ACT OF GOD.
(THESE THREE SPECIFIC ACTS OF THE DEITY
MAY FURNISH THE CLERGY WITH A TEXT.)
I AM CLEAR IN MY PURPOSE TO REMOVE
THE PRESIDENT. TWO POINTS WILL BE
ACCOMPLISHED: IT WILL SAVE THE
REPUBLIC, AND IT WILL CREATE A
DEMAND FOR MY BOOK, "THE TRUTH."
HIS BOOK WAS NOT WRITTEN FOR MONEY.
AS WRITTEN TO SAVE SOULS. IN ORDER
RACT PUBLIC ATTENTION, THE BOO
RS THE NOTICE THE PRESID
WILL GIVE IT.
C.G.

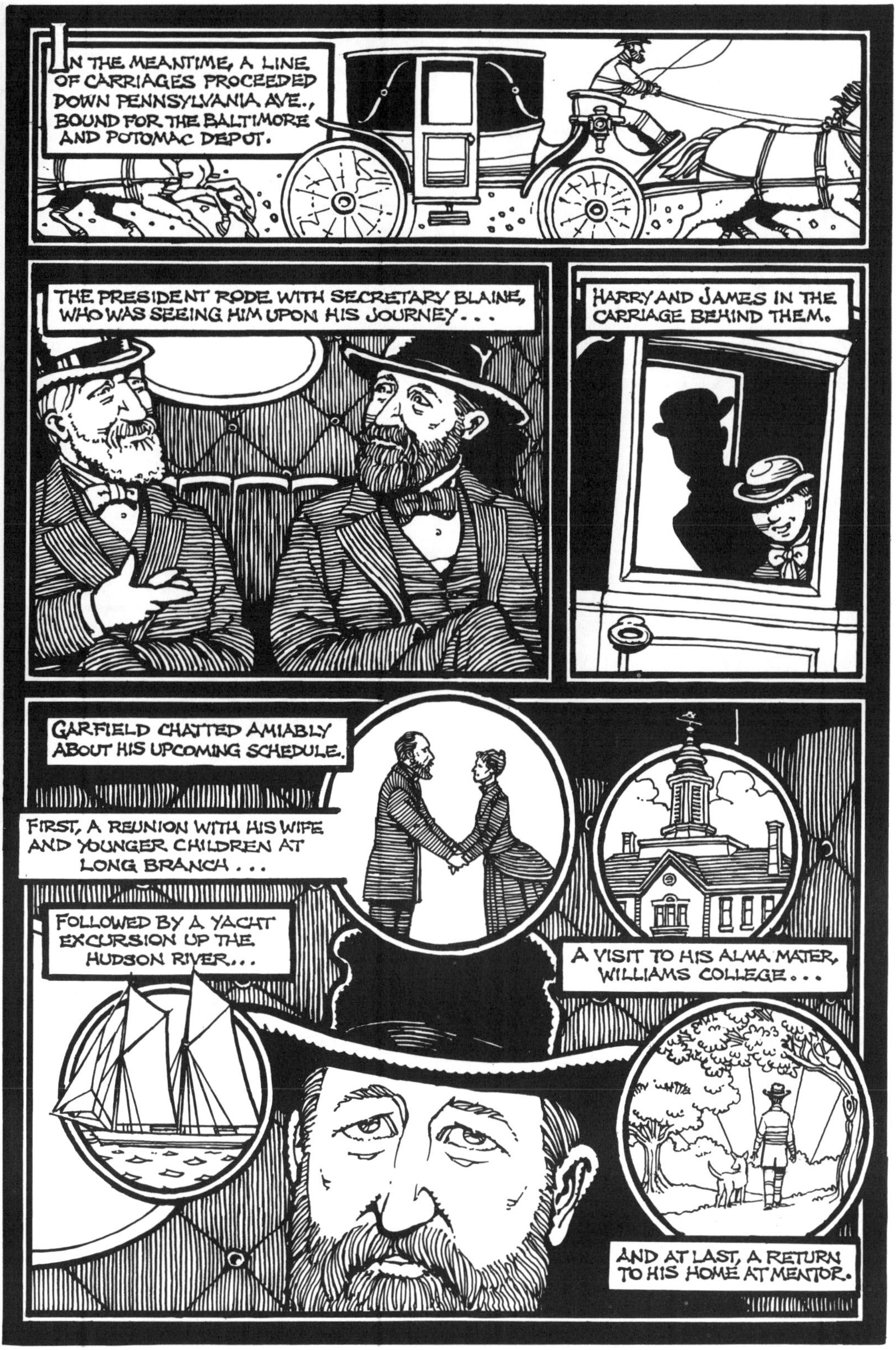
IN THE MEANTIME, A LINE OF CARRIAGES PROCEEDED DOWN PENNSYLVANIA AVE., BOUND FOR THE BALTIMORE AND POTOMAC DEPOT.
THE PRESIDENT RODE WITH SECRETARY BLAINE, WHO WAS SEEING HIM UPON HIS JOURNEY . . .
HARRY AND JAMES IN THE CARRIAGE BEHIND THEM.
GARFIELD CHATTED AMIABLY ABOUT HIS UPCOMING SCHEDULE.
FIRST, A REUNION WITH HIS WIFE AND YOUNGER CHILDREN AT LONG BRANCH . . .
FOLLOWED BY A YACHT EXCURSION UP THE HUDSON RIVER . . .
A VISIT TO HIS ALMA MATER, WILLIAMS COLLEGE . . .
AND AT LAST, A RETURN TO HIS HOME AT MENTOR.

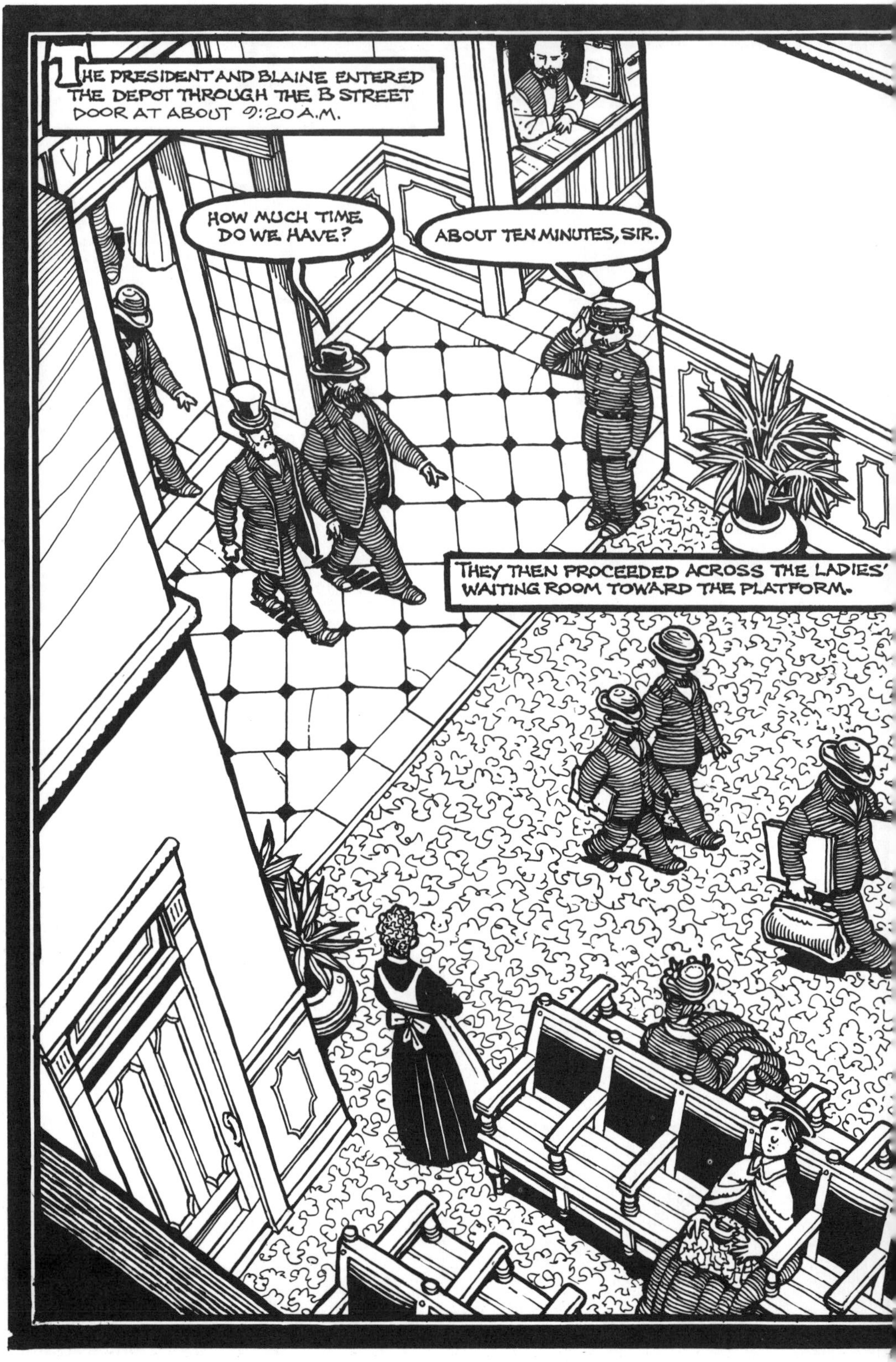
THE PRESIDENT AND BLAINE ENTERED THE DEPOT THROUGH THE B STREET DOOR AT ABOUT 9:20 A.M.
HOW MUCH TIME DO WE HAVE?
ABOUT TEN MINUTES, SIR.
THEY THEN PROCEEDED ACROSS THE LADIES' WAITING ROOM TOWARD THE PLATFORM.

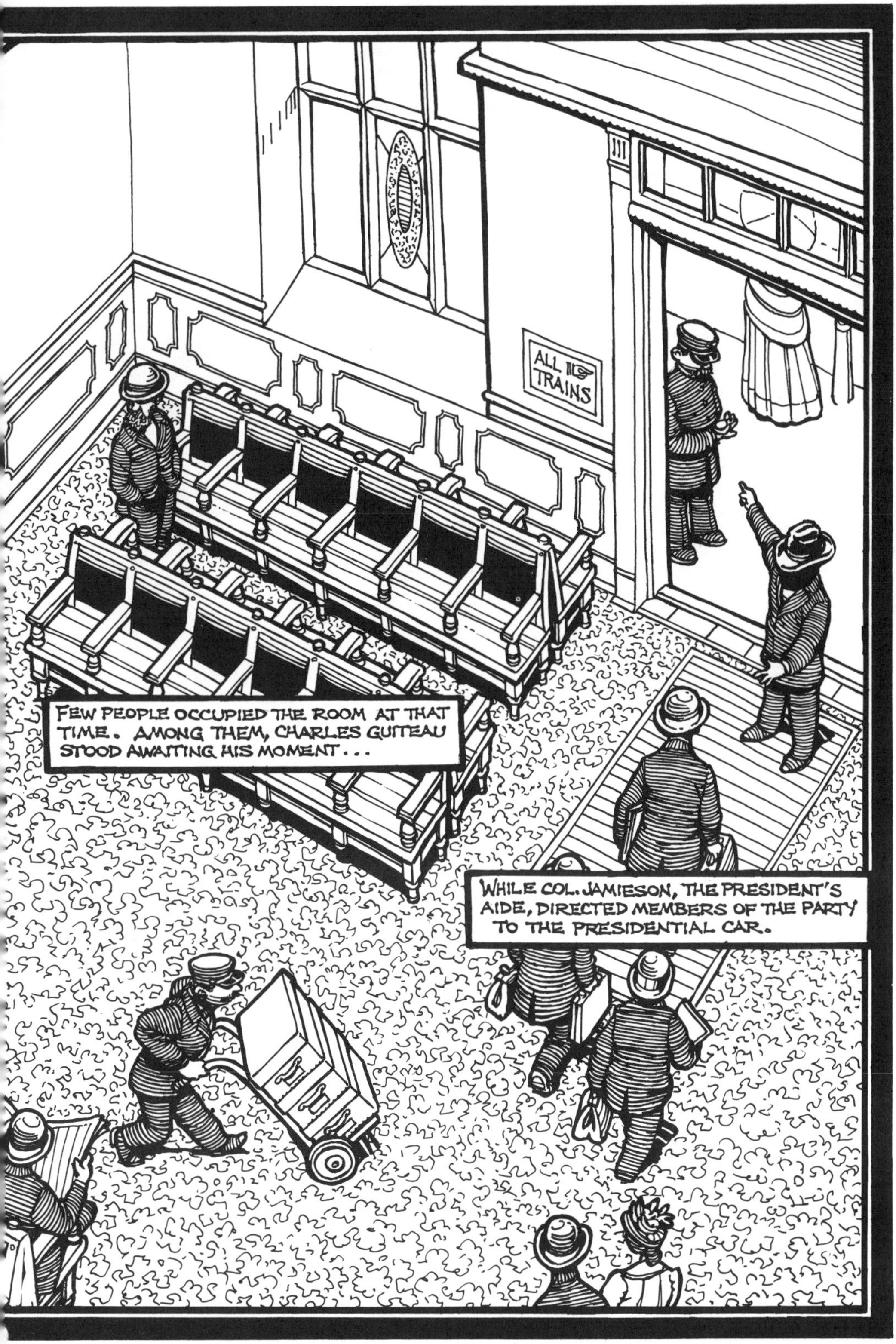
ALL TRAINS
FEW PEOPLE OCCUPIED THE ROOM AT THAT TIME. AMONG THEM, CHARLES GUITEAU STOOD AWAITING HIS MOMENT...
WHILE COL. JAMIESON, THE PRESIDENT'S AIDE, DIRECTED MEMBERS OF THE PARTY TO THE PRESIDENTIAL CAR.

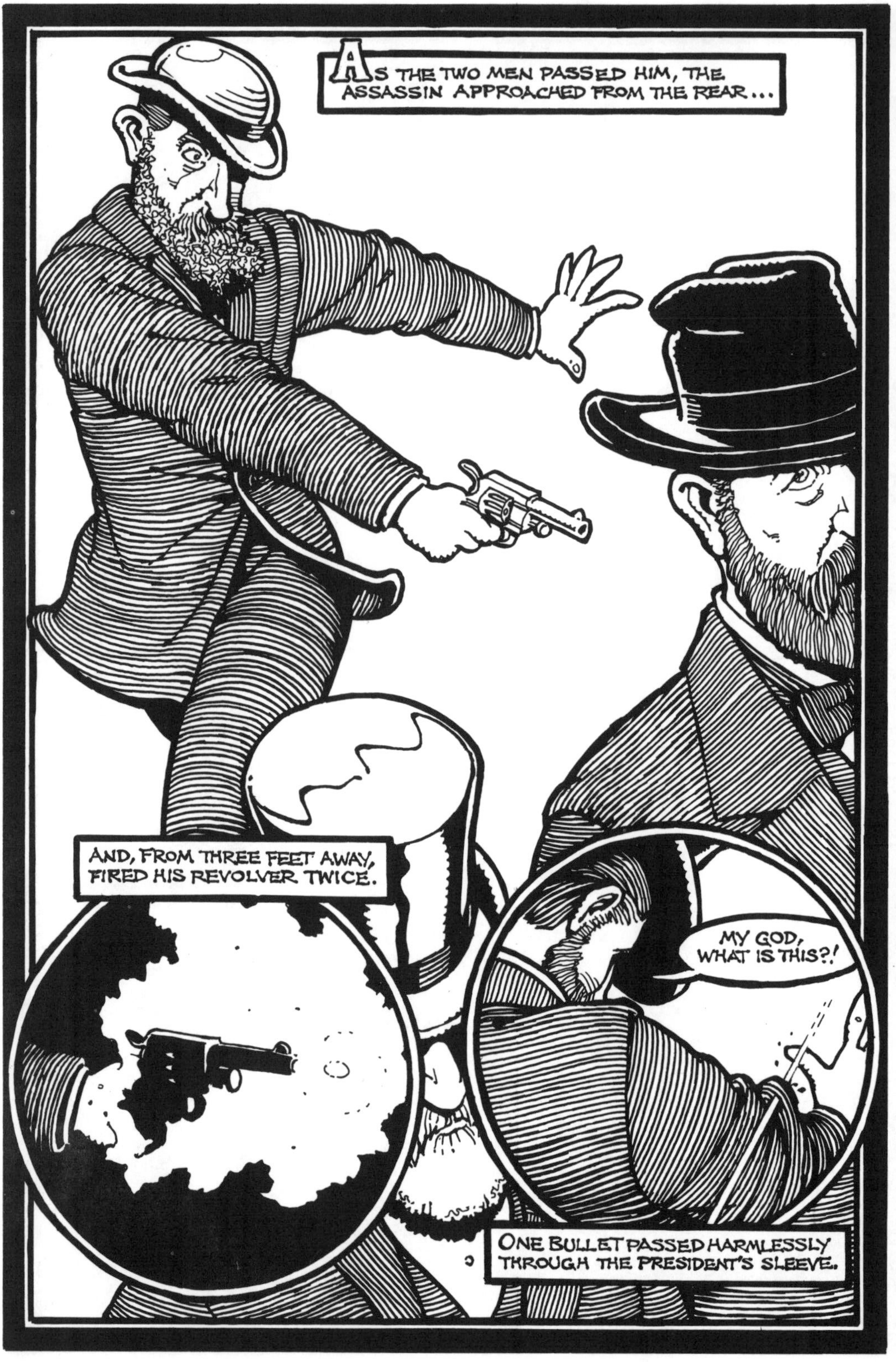
AS THE TWO MEN PASSED HIM, THE ASSASSIN APPROACHED FROM THE REAR...
AND, FROM THREE FEET AWAY, FIRED HIS REVOLVER TWICE.
MY GOD, WHAT IS THIS?!
ONE BULLET PASSED HARMLESSLY THROUGH THE PRESIDENT'S SLEEVE.

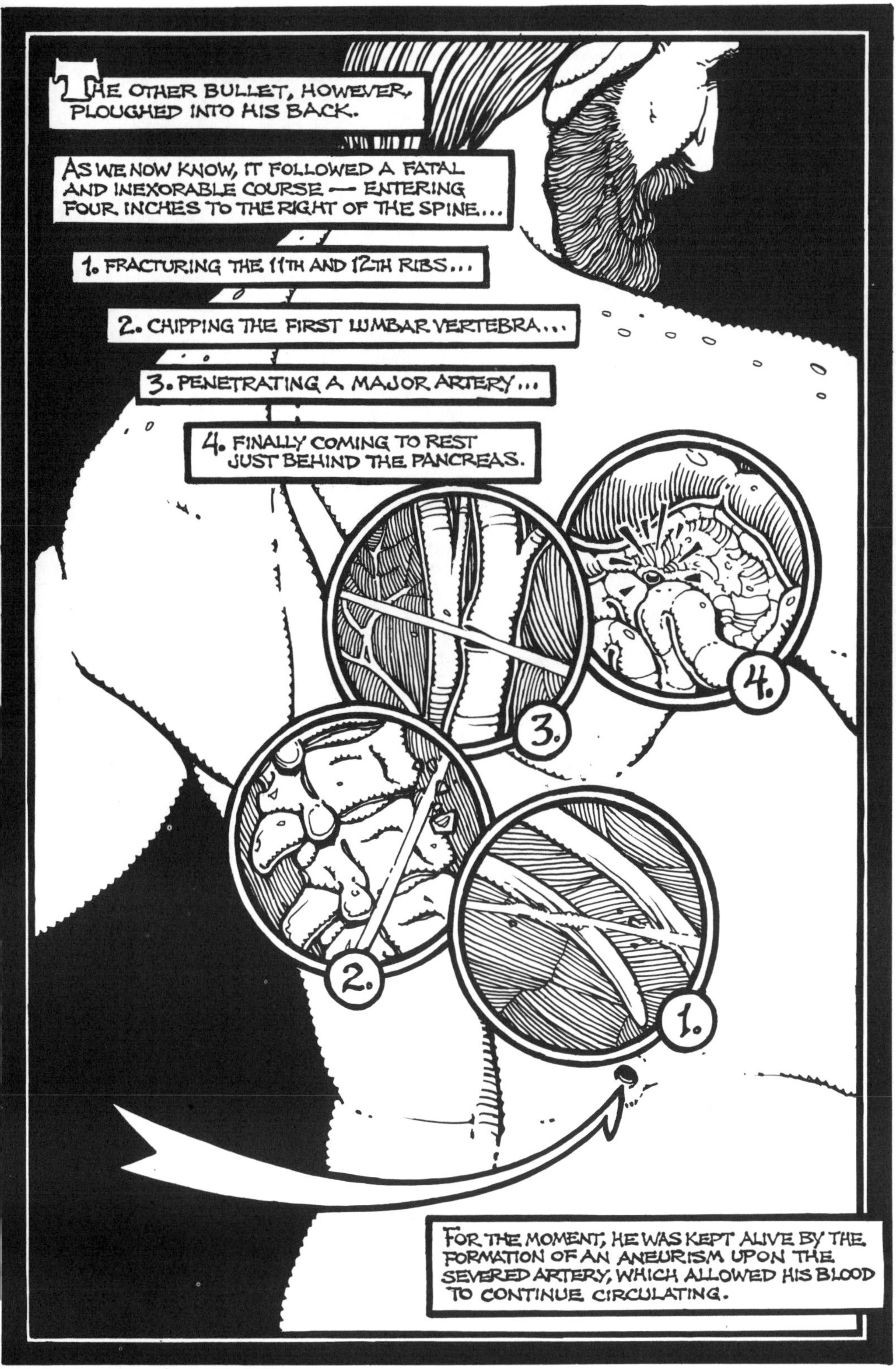
THE OTHER BULLET, HOWEVER, PLOUGHED INTO HIS BACK.
AS WE NOW KNOW, IT FOLLOWED A FATAL AND INEXORABLE COURSE — ENTERING FOUR INCHES TO THE RIGHT OF THE SPINE...
1. FRACTURING THE 11TH AND 12TH RIBS...
2. CHIPPING THE FIRST LUMBAR VERTEBRA...
3. PENETRATING A MAJOR ARTERY...
4. FINALLY COMING TO REST JUST BEHIND THE PANCREAS.
3.
4.
2.
1.
FOR THE MOMENT, HE WAS KEPT ALIVE BY THE FORMATION OF AN ANEURISM UPON THE SEVERED ARTERY, WHICH ALLOWED HIS BLOOD TO CONTINUE CIRCULATING.

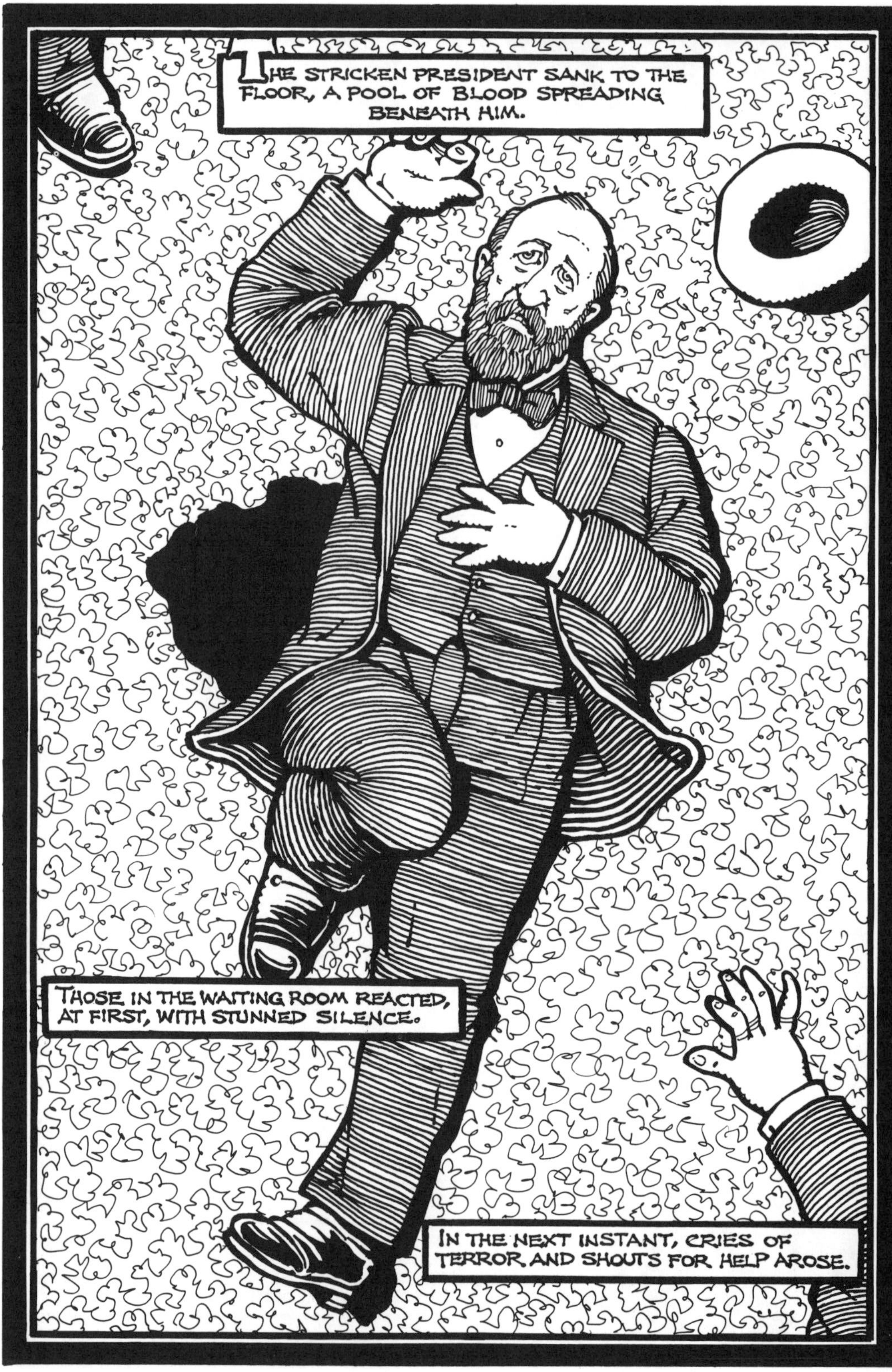
THE STRICKEN PRESIDENT SANK TO THE FLOOR, A POOL OF BLOOD SPREADING BENEATH HIM.
THOSE IN THE WAITING ROOM REACTED, AT FIRST, WITH STUNNED SILENCE.
IN THE NEXT INSTANT, CRIES OF TERROR AND SHOUTS FOR HELP AROSE.

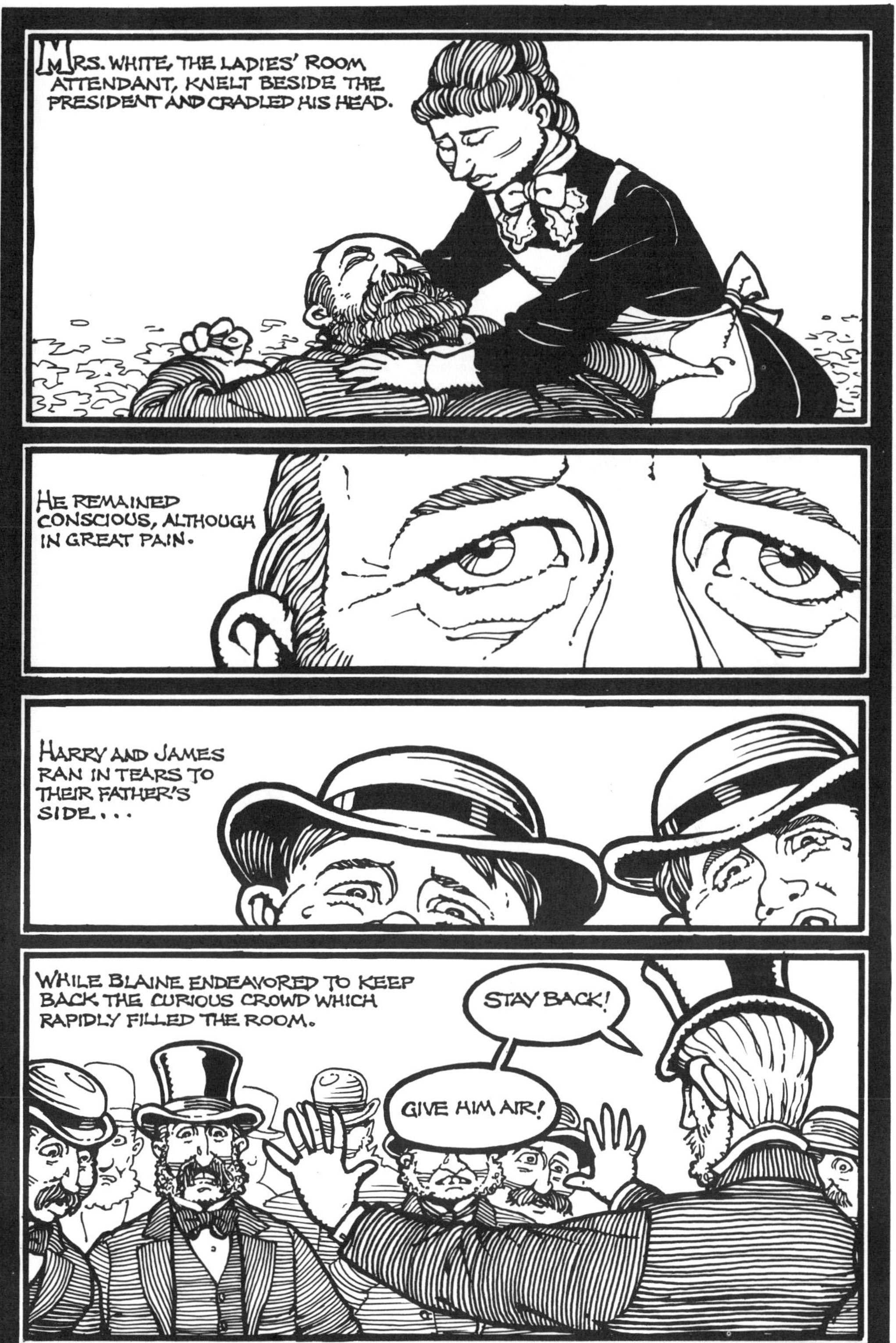
MRS. WHITE, THE LADIES' ROOM ATTENDANT, KNELT BESIDE THE PRESIDENT AND CRADLED HIS HEAD.
HE REMAINED CONSCIOUS, ALTHOUGH IN GREAT PAIN.
HARRY AND JAMES RAN IN TEARS TO THEIR FATHER'S SIDE . . .
WHILE BLAINE ENDEAVORED TO KEEP BACK THE CURIOUS CROWD WHICH RAPIDLY FILLED THE ROOM.
STAY BACK!
GIVE HIM AIR!

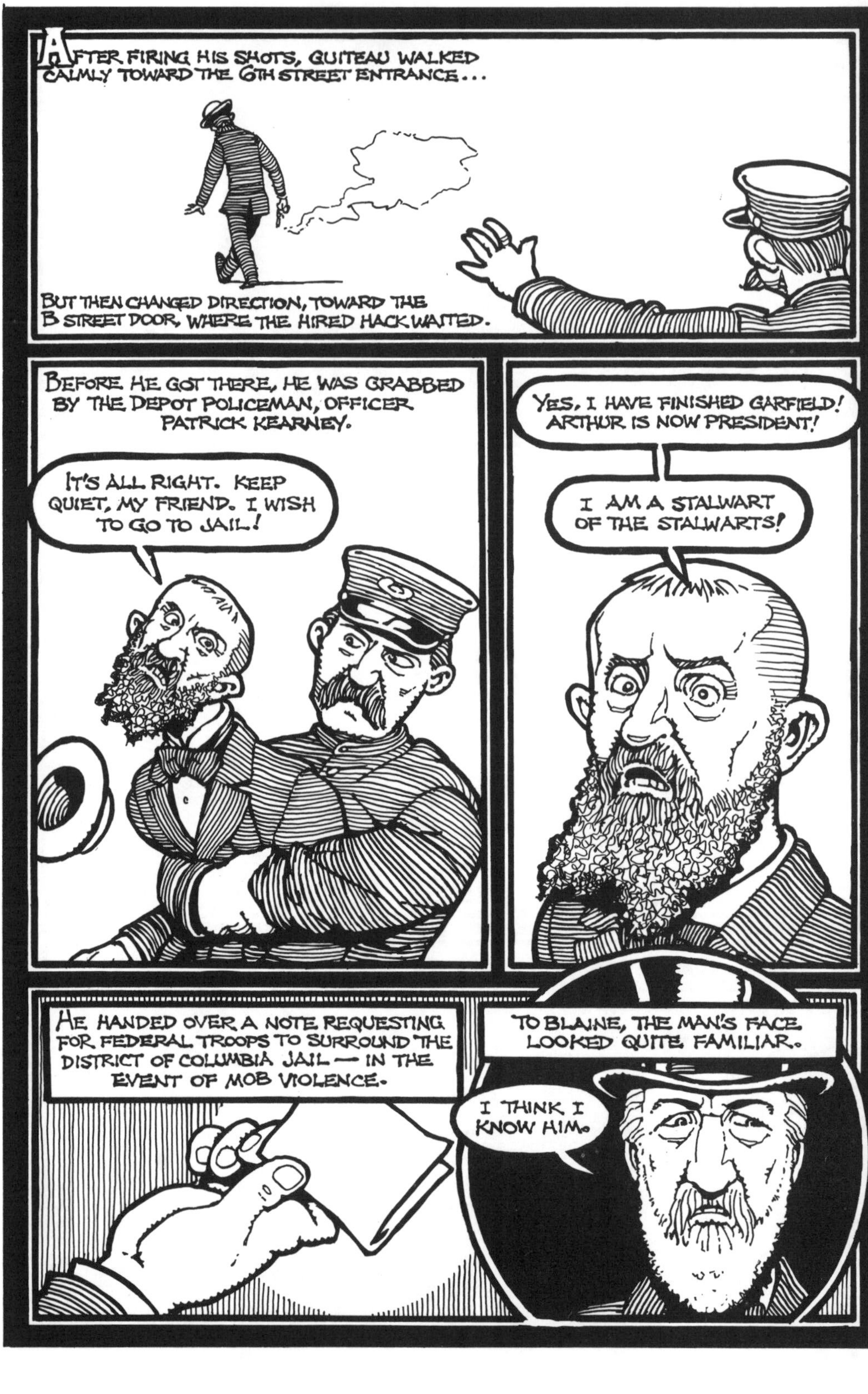
After firing his shots, Guiteau walked calmly toward the 6th street entrance...
But then changed direction, toward the B street door, where the hired hack waited.
Before he got there, he was grabbed by the depot policeman, officer Patrick Kearney.
It's all right. Keep quiet, my friend. I wish to go to jail!
Yes, I have finished Garfield! Arthur is now president!
I am a stalwart of the stalwarts!
He handed over a note requesting for federal troops to surround the District of Columbia jail — in the event of mob violence.
To Blaine, the man's face looked quite familiar.
I think I know him.

THE ASSASSIN GREW NERVOUS AS THE CROWD BEGAN TO PRESS TOWARD HIM.

LYNCH HIM!

BUT AT LAST, OFFICERS OF THE METROPOLITAN POLICE FORCE ARRIVED...

AND GUITEAU WAS WHISKED OUT THE B STREET DOOR AND INTO A POLICE VAN.

BACK INSIDE THE DEPOT, AMID THE STEADILY-GROWING MASS OF PEOPLE, THE PRESIDENT WAS LIFTED CLUMSILY ONTO A MATTRESS...

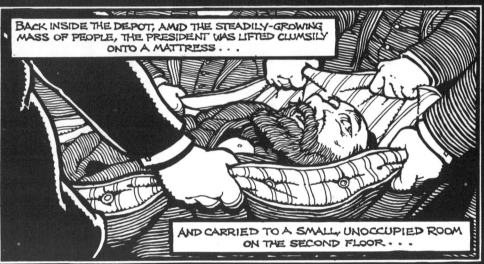

AND CARRIED TO A SMALL, UNOCCUPIED ROOM ON THE SECOND FLOOR...

AT THIS POINT, THE FIRST PHYSICIAN ARRIVED: DR. E.W. BLISS, A LONG-TIME FRIEND OF THE PRESIDENT.

HE EXAMINED THE WOUND AND EXPRESSED A HOPEFUL PROGNOSIS. THE PATIENT, HOWEVER, CONTRADICTED HIM!

THANK YOU, DOCTOR, BUT I AM A DEAD MAN.

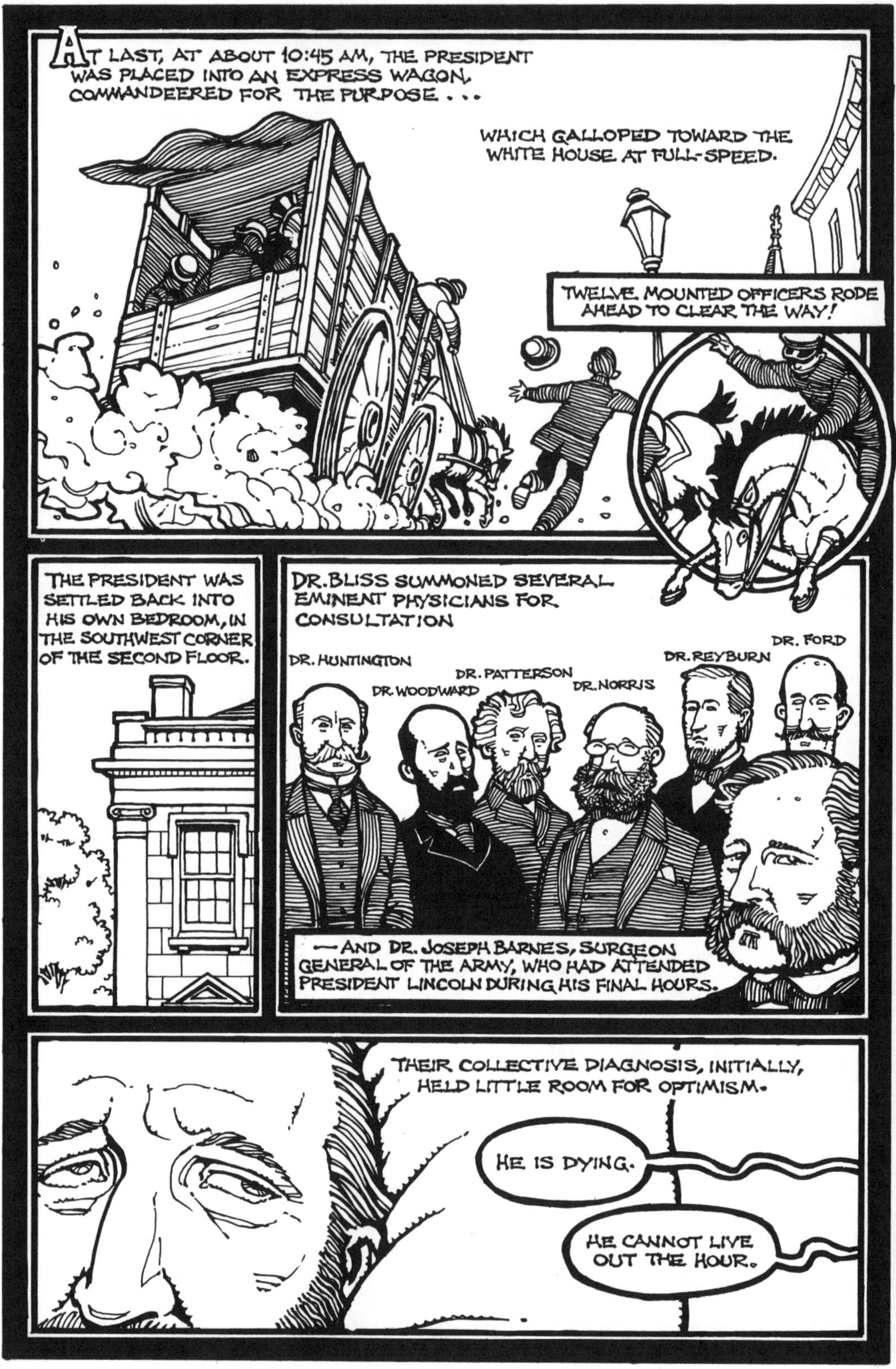
AT LAST, AT ABOUT 10:45 AM, THE PRESIDENT WAS PLACED INTO AN EXPRESS WAGON, COMMANDEERED FOR THE PURPOSE . . .
WHICH GALLOPED TOWARD THE WHITE HOUSE AT FULL-SPEED.
TWELVE MOUNTED OFFICERS RODE AHEAD TO CLEAR THE WAY!
THE PRESIDENT WAS SETTLED BACK INTO HIS OWN BEDROOM, IN THE SOUTHWEST CORNER OF THE SECOND FLOOR.
DR. BLISS SUMMONED SEVERAL EMINENT PHYSICIANS FOR CONSULTATION
DR. HUNTINGTON
DR. WOODWARD
DR. PATTERSON
DR. NORRIS
DR. REYBURN
DR. FORD
—AND DR. JOSEPH BARNES, SURGEON GENERAL OF THE ARMY, WHO HAD ATTENDED PRESIDENT LINCOLN DURING HIS FINAL HOURS.
THEIR COLLECTIVE DIAGNOSIS, INITIALLY, HELD LITTLE ROOM FOR OPTIMISM.
HE IS DYING.
HE CANNOT LIVE OUT THE HOUR.

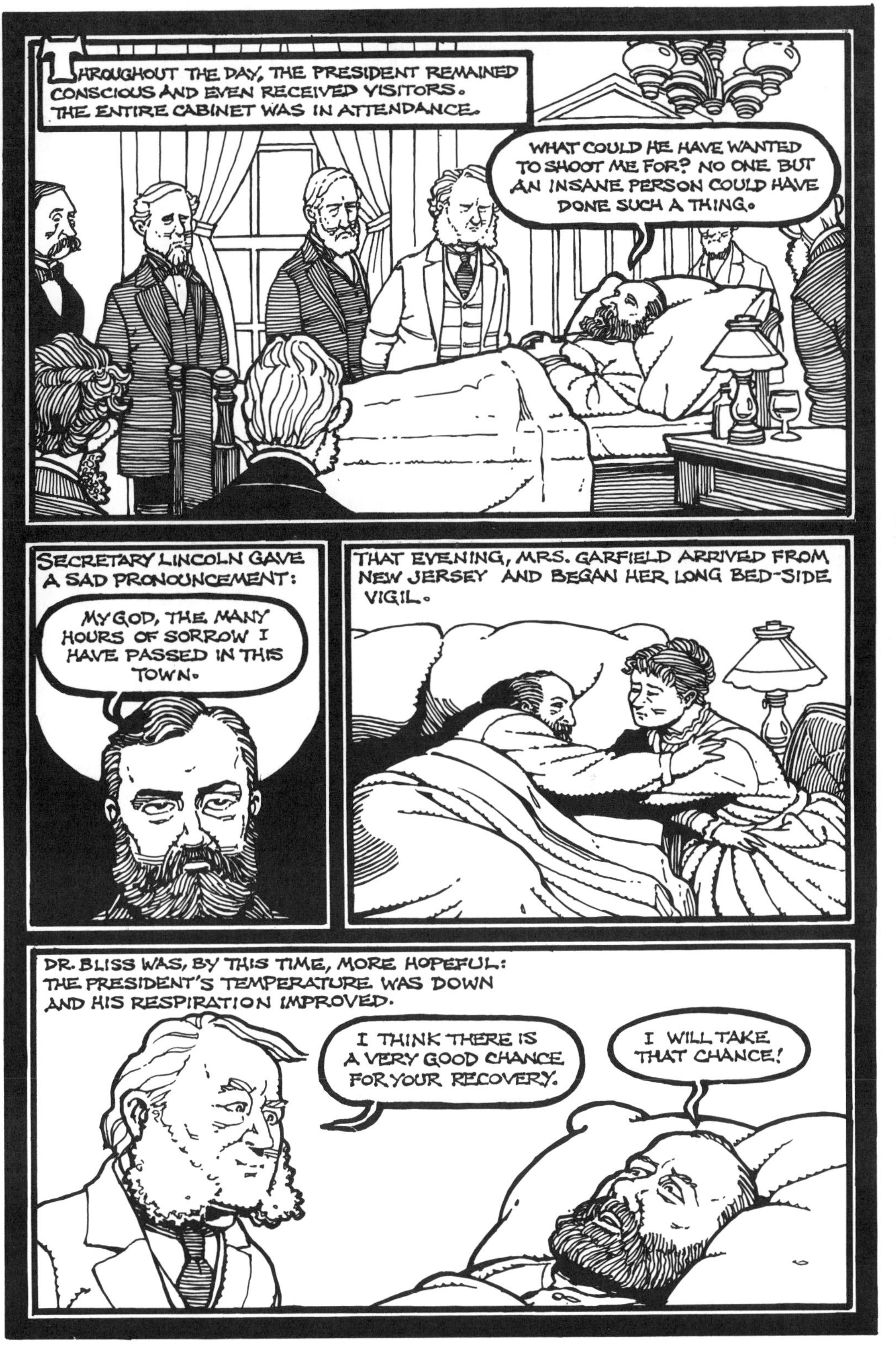
THROUGHOUT THE DAY, THE PRESIDENT REMAINED CONSCIOUS AND EVEN RECEIVED VISITORS. THE ENTIRE CABINET WAS IN ATTENDANCE.
WHAT COULD HE HAVE WANTED TO SHOOT ME FOR? NO ONE BUT AN INSANE PERSON COULD HAVE DONE SUCH A THING.
SECRETARY LINCOLN GAVE A SAD PRONOUNCEMENT:
MY GOD, THE MANY HOURS OF SORROW I HAVE PASSED IN THIS TOWN.
THAT EVENING, MRS. GARFIELD ARRIVED FROM NEW JERSEY AND BEGAN HER LONG BED-SIDE VIGIL.
DR. BLISS WAS, BY THIS TIME, MORE HOPEFUL: THE PRESIDENT'S TEMPERATURE WAS DOWN AND HIS RESPIRATION IMPROVED.
I THINK THERE IS A VERY GOOD CHANCE FOR YOUR RECOVERY.
I WILL TAKE THAT CHANCE!

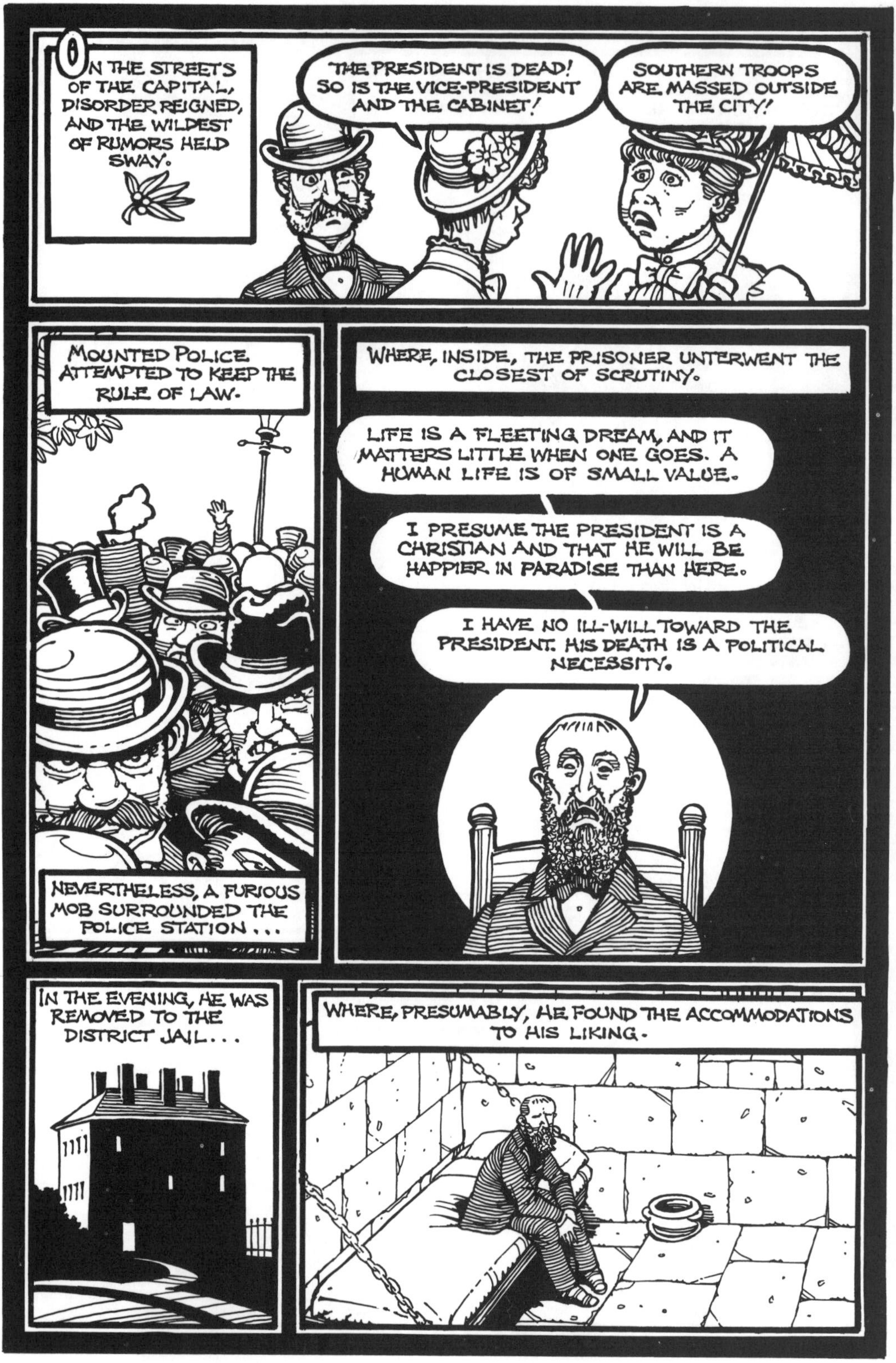
ON THE STREETS OF THE CAPITAL, DISORDER REIGNED, AND THE WILDEST OF RUMORS HELD SWAY.
THE PRESIDENT IS DEAD! SO IS THE VICE-PRESIDENT AND THE CABINET!
SOUTHERN TROOPS ARE MASSED OUTSIDE THE CITY!
MOUNTED POLICE ATTEMPTED TO KEEP THE RULE OF LAW.
NEVERTHELESS, A FURIOUS MOB SURROUNDED THE POLICE STATION . . .
WHERE, INSIDE, THE PRISONER UNTERWENT THE CLOSEST OF SCRUTINY.
LIFE IS A FLEETING DREAM, AND IT MATTERS LITTLE WHEN ONE GOES. A HUMAN LIFE IS OF SMALL VALUE.
I PRESUME THE PRESIDENT IS A CHRISTIAN AND THAT HE WILL BE HAPPIER IN PARADISE THAN HERE.
I HAVE NO ILL-WILL TOWARD THE PRESIDENT. HIS DEATH IS A POLITICAL NECESSITY.
IN THE EVENING, HE WAS REMOVED TO THE DISTRICT JAIL . . .
WHERE, PRESUMABLY, HE FOUND THE ACCOMMODATIONS TO HIS LIKING.

PART III.
THE LONG SUMMER.

IN WHICH AN ANXIOUS NATION
FOLLOWS THE UNCERTAIN COURSE
OF THEIR LEADER'S FATE.

As the month of July progressed, the public was kept informed of the president's condition by official bulletins issued several times daily.

HYDNUTS DRUGGIST

OFFICIAL BULLETIN– 12:30 P.M. The president has been tranquil and has not vomited since morning bulletin, but has not yet rallied from the prostration of yesterday afternoon as much as was hoped. The enemata administered are however still retained. At present his pulse is 114, temp. 98.3, respiration 18.

...CIAL BULLETIN 7 P.M. The president's symp... still grave yet he seems to have lost no ...d during the day. His condition on the ...is rather better than yesterday. He vomited ...nce during the day. At present, his pulse ...s 120, temp. 98.5, respiration 19.

At the White House, messages and gifts arrived from around the world . . .

As well as a wide array of home remedies and quack medicines.

Mrs. Garfield supervised the patient's diet and prepared special dishes herself.

Dr. Bliss called in several more medical consultants . . .

DR. HAMILTON

DR. AGNEW

DR. BOYNTON

And the noted "homeopath" Dr. Susan Edson.

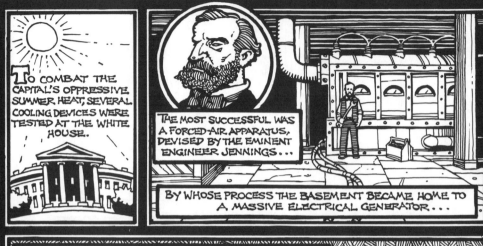

TO COMBAT THE CAPITAL'S OPPRESSIVE SUMMER HEAT, SEVERAL COOLING DEVICES WERE TESTED AT THE WHITE HOUSE.

THE MOST SUCCESSFUL WAS A FORCED-AIR APPARATUS, DEVISED BY THE EMINENT ENGINEER JENNINGS...

BY WHOSE PROCESS THE BASEMENT BECAME HOME TO A MASSIVE ELECTRICAL GENERATOR...

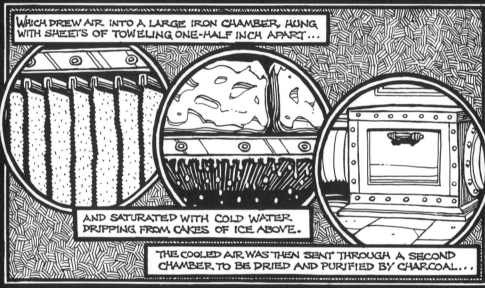

WHICH DREW AIR INTO A LARGE IRON CHAMBER, HUNG WITH SHEETS OF TOWELING ONE-HALF INCH APART...

AND SATURATED WITH COLD WATER DRIPPING FROM CAKES OF ICE ABOVE.

THE COOLED AIR WAS THEN SENT THROUGH A SECOND CHAMBER TO BE DRIED AND PURIFIED BY CHARCOAL...

AND THEN INTO THE PRESIDENT'S BEDROOM, KEEPING IT TO A RELATIVE COMFORT.

THE CORPS OF PHYSICIANS IN ATTENDANCE, HOWEVER, WERE LESS SUCCESSFUL IN THE TREATMENT OF THEIR PATIENT.

DR. BLISS, AT ONE POINT, ATTEMPTED TO LOCATE THE BULLET BY MEANS OF A "NELATION PROBE."

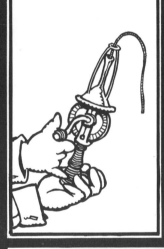

WHICH WAS PUSHED INTO THE WOUND AND TURNED UNTIL IT COULD DISCOVER THE BULLET'S PATH.

ASIDE FROM CAUSING GREAT PAIN TO THE PRESIDENT, THE DEVICE FAILED TO LOCATE THE BULLET...

BUT SUCCEEDED, AS IT TURNED OUT, IN GREATLY ENLARGING THE WOUND, AND INCREASING THE CHANCE OF INFECTION.

EACH DOCTOR, IN HIS TURN, PROBED THE OPENING WITH A BARE FINGER (TO THE POINT, AT LAST, OF PUNCTURING THE PRESIDENT'S LIVER!)

OPINION AS TO THE BULLET'S LOCATION WAS LIKELY TO VARY DAY-TO-DAY.

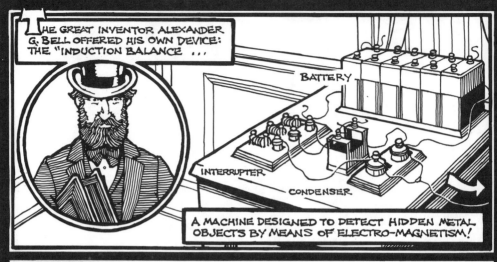

THE GREAT INVENTOR ALEXANDER G. BELL OFFERED HIS OWN DEVICE: THE "INDUCTION BALANCE" ...

BATTERY

INTERRUPTER

CONDENSER

A MACHINE DESIGNED TO DETECT HIDDEN METAL OBJECTS BY MEANS OF ELECTRO-MAGNETISM!

SEVERAL TESTS WERE MADE UPON THE PRESIDENT, WHO WATCHED WITH GREAT INTEREST.

THE DEVICE AT LENGTH CONCLUDED THAT THE BULLET LAY TO THE FRONT OF THE STOMACH ...

WHICH ASSESSMENT, OF COURSE, WAS LATER SHOWN TO BE IN ERROR.

THE PHYSICIANS, IN ANY CASE, AGREED NOT TO FURTHER EXPLORE THE PRESIDENT'S WOUND.

CHARLES GUITEAU, IN THE MEANTIME, WAS ENJOYING THE LIFE OF HIS DREAMS IN HIS SMALL CELL AT THE DISTRICT JAIL.

HE WAS ALLOWED VISITS FROM FAMILY MEMBERS, AS WELL AS FROM THE OCCASIONAL JOURNALIST.

LETTERS OF PRAISE AND SUPPORT ARRIVED DAILY.

MOST GRATIFYING OF ALL, HIS WRITINGS WERE NOW PUBLISHED FAR AND WIDE, BRINGING HIM HIS LARGEST AUDIENCE EVER.

The Life and Theology of Charles J. Guiteau

prepared by Himself

HE WORKED DILIGENTLY EVERY DAY UPON HIS MEMOIRS.

HE SAW NO NEED TO CONSULT WITH LAWYERS, BEING CERTAIN THAT HIS DEFENSE WOULD TAKE CARE OF ITSELF.

IN FACT, HE FULLY EXPECTED THAT SUCH STALWARTS AS GEN. GRANT, SENATOR CONKLING AND VICE-PRESIDENT ARTHUR WOULD SEE THAT NO HARM CAME TO HIM.

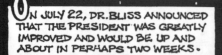
ON JULY 22, DR. BLISS ANNOUNCED THAT THE PRESIDENT WAS GREATLY IMPROVED AND WOULD BE UP AND ABOUT IN PERHAPS TWO WEEKS.

BUT ON THE VERY NEXT DAY, THE PATIENT CAUGHT A SEVERE CHILL AND TOOK A TURN FOR THE WORSE.

ON JULY 29, HE WAS WELL ENOUGH TO PRESIDE OVER A CABINET MEETING AT HIS BED-SIDE.

HIS CONDITION WORSENED INTO THE MONTH OF AUGUST.

RALLYING AGAIN ON AUGUST 10, HE SIGNED ONE OFFICIAL DOCUMENT...

AND COMPOSED A FEW WORDS OF COMFORT TO HIS MOTHER IN OHIO (HIS LAST LETTER, AS IT TURNED OUT):

DEAR MOTHER —
DON'T BE DISTURBED BY CONFLICTING REPORTS ABOUT MY CONDITION. IT IS TRUE I AM STILL WEAK AND ON MY BACK, BUT I AM GAINING EVERY DAY AND NEED ONLY TIME AND PATIENCE TO BRING ME THROUGH. GIVE MY LOVE TO ALL THE RELATIVES AND FRIENDS. YOUR LOVING SON,
James A. Garfield

BY THIS TIME, THE PRESIDENT'S PHYSICAL APPEARANCE HAD ALTERED MARKEDLY: HIS WEIGHT HAD DROPPED FROM A STRAPPING 205 lbs. TO A MERE 130.

IN EARLY SEPTEMBER, AS A LAST HOPE, IT WAS DECIDED THAT A CHANGE OF ATMOSPHERE MIGHT BE IN ORDER.

ON SEPTEMBER 6 — THE HOTTEST DAY OF THE YEAR — THE PRESIDENT WAS PLACED IN A SPECIALLY-FITTED RAILWAY CAR...

AND TAKEN NORTH — TO THE SEA-SHORE AT ELBERON, NEW JERSEY.

PENN.

N.J.

MD.

DEL.

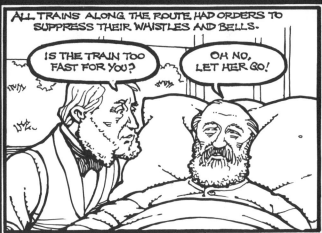

ALL TRAINS ALONG THE ROUTE HAD ORDERS TO SUPPRESS THEIR WHISTLES AND BELLS.

IS THE TRAIN TOO FAST FOR YOU?

OH NO, LET HER GO!

A SPECIAL SPUR WAS LAID THAT BROUGHT THE CAR DIRECTLY TO THE 20-ROOM HOUSE PLACED AT THE PRESIDENT'S DISPOSAL BY MR. CHARLES FRANCKLYN.

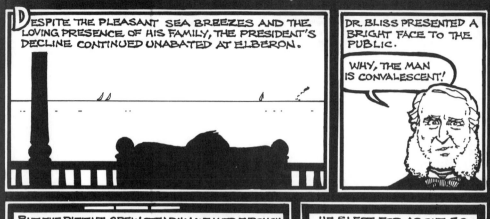

DESPITE THE PLEASANT SEA BREEZES AND THE LOVING PRESENCE OF HIS FAMILY, THE PRESIDENT'S DECLINE CONTINUED UNABATED AT ELBERON.

DR. BLISS PRESENTED A BRIGHT FACE TO THE PUBLIC.

WHY, THE MAN IS CONVALESCENT!

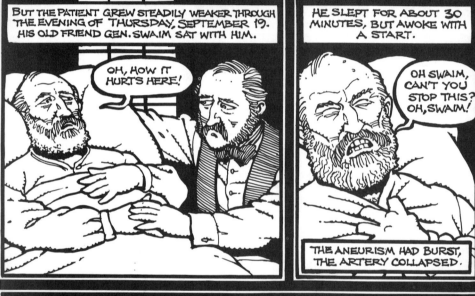

BUT THE PATIENT GREW STEADILY WEAKER THROUGH THE EVENING OF THURSDAY, SEPTEMBER 19. HIS OLD FRIEND GEN. SWAIM SAT WITH HIM.

OH, HOW IT HURTS HERE!

HE SLEPT FOR ABOUT 30 MINUTES, BUT AWOKE WITH A START.

OH SWAIM, CAN'T YOU STOP THIS? OH, SWAIM!

THE ANEURISM HAD BURST, THE ARTERY COLLAPSED.

AT 10:35 PM, WITH HIS FAMILY AROUND HIM, GARFIELD BREATHED HIS LAST.

IT IS OVER.

CONCLUSION:
AT THE BAR OF JUSTICE

IN WHICH THE NATION RECEIVES A GLIMPSE INTO THE HEART OF EVIL.

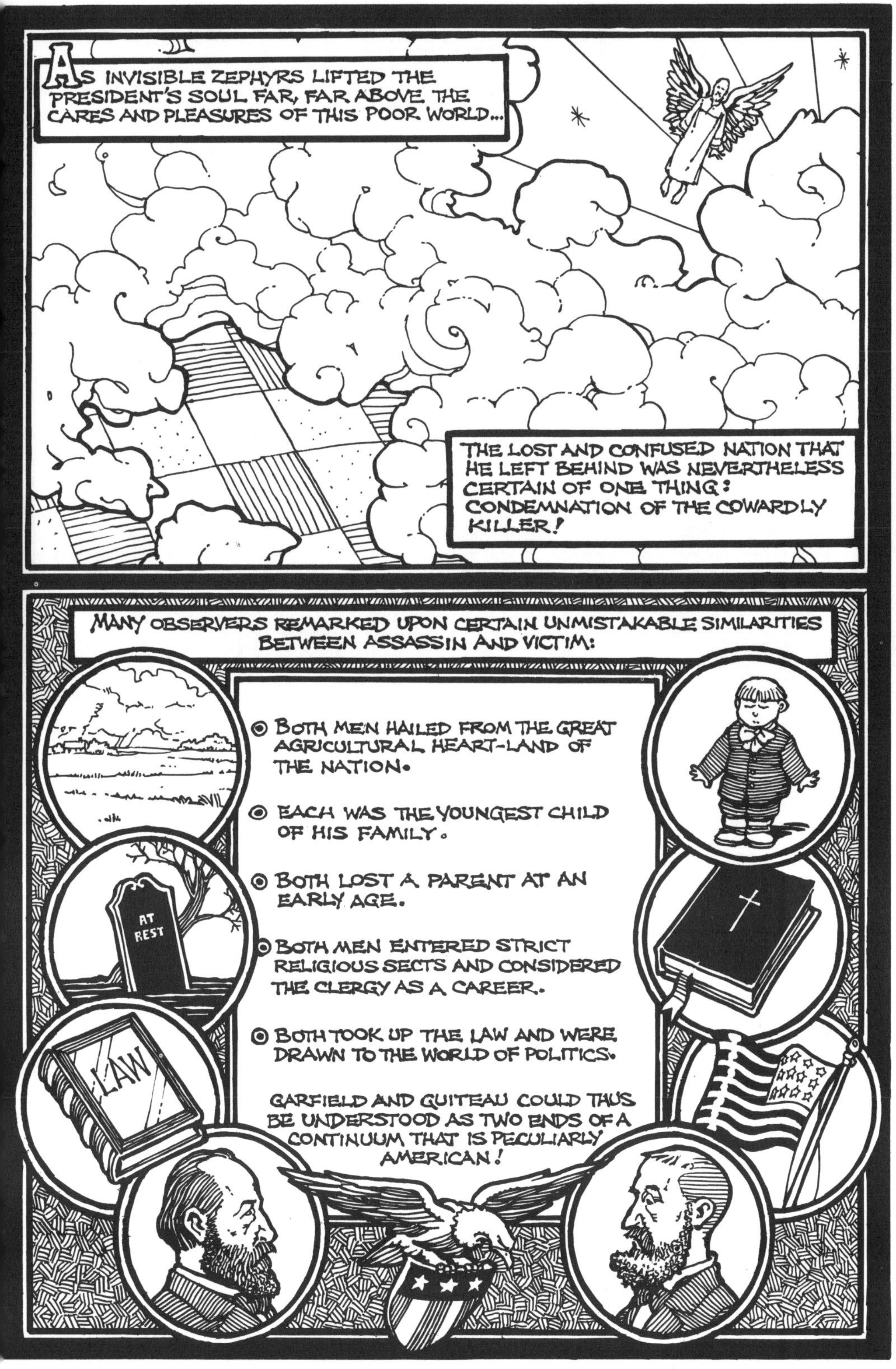
AS INVISIBLE ZEPHYRS LIFTED THE PRESIDENT'S SOUL FAR, FAR ABOVE THE CARES AND PLEASURES OF THIS POOR WORLD...
THE LOST AND CONFUSED NATION THAT HE LEFT BEHIND WAS NEVERTHELESS CERTAIN OF ONE THING: CONDEMNATION OF THE COWARDLY KILLER!
MANY OBSERVERS REMARKED UPON CERTAIN UNMISTAKABLE SIMILARITIES BETWEEN ASSASSIN AND VICTIM:
BOTH MEN HAILED FROM THE GREAT AGRICULTURAL HEART-LAND OF THE NATION.
EACH WAS THE YOUNGEST CHILD OF HIS FAMILY.
BOTH LOST A PARENT AT AN EARLY AGE.
BOTH MEN ENTERED STRICT RELIGIOUS SECTS AND CONSIDERED THE CLERGY AS A CAREER.
BOTH TOOK UP THE LAW AND WERE DRAWN TO THE WORLD OF POLITICS.
GARFIELD AND GUITEAU COULD THUS BE UNDERSTOOD AS TWO ENDS OF A CONTINUUM THAT IS PECULIARLY AMERICAN!
AT REST
LAW

NOVEMBER 14, 1881 CHARLES GUITEAU WAS AT LAST BROUGHT TO TRIAL BEFORE THE SUPREME COURT OF THE DISTRICT OF COLUMBIA.

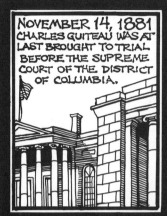

JUDGE WALTER S. COX PRESIDING.

SOCIETY LUMINARIES MINGLED WITH RIFF-RAFF IN THE PACKED COURT-ROOM.

ON THE OPENING DAY, THE DEFENDANT ADDRESSED THE COURT DIRECTLY, THUS SETTING THE TONE FOR THE PROCEEDINGS TO COME.

I COME HERE IN THE CAPACITY OF AN AGENT OF THE DEITY IN THIS MATTER.

THE GOVERNMENT PRESENTED A FORMIDABLE CHAIN OF WITNESSES AGAINST THE DEFENDANT — AMONG THEM HIS FORMER WIFE!

ALL OF THEM WERE SUBJECT TO CONSTANT INTERRUPTION:

WHY YOU OLD HOG!

LOW, DIRTY LIAR!

VILLAIN! VILLAIN!

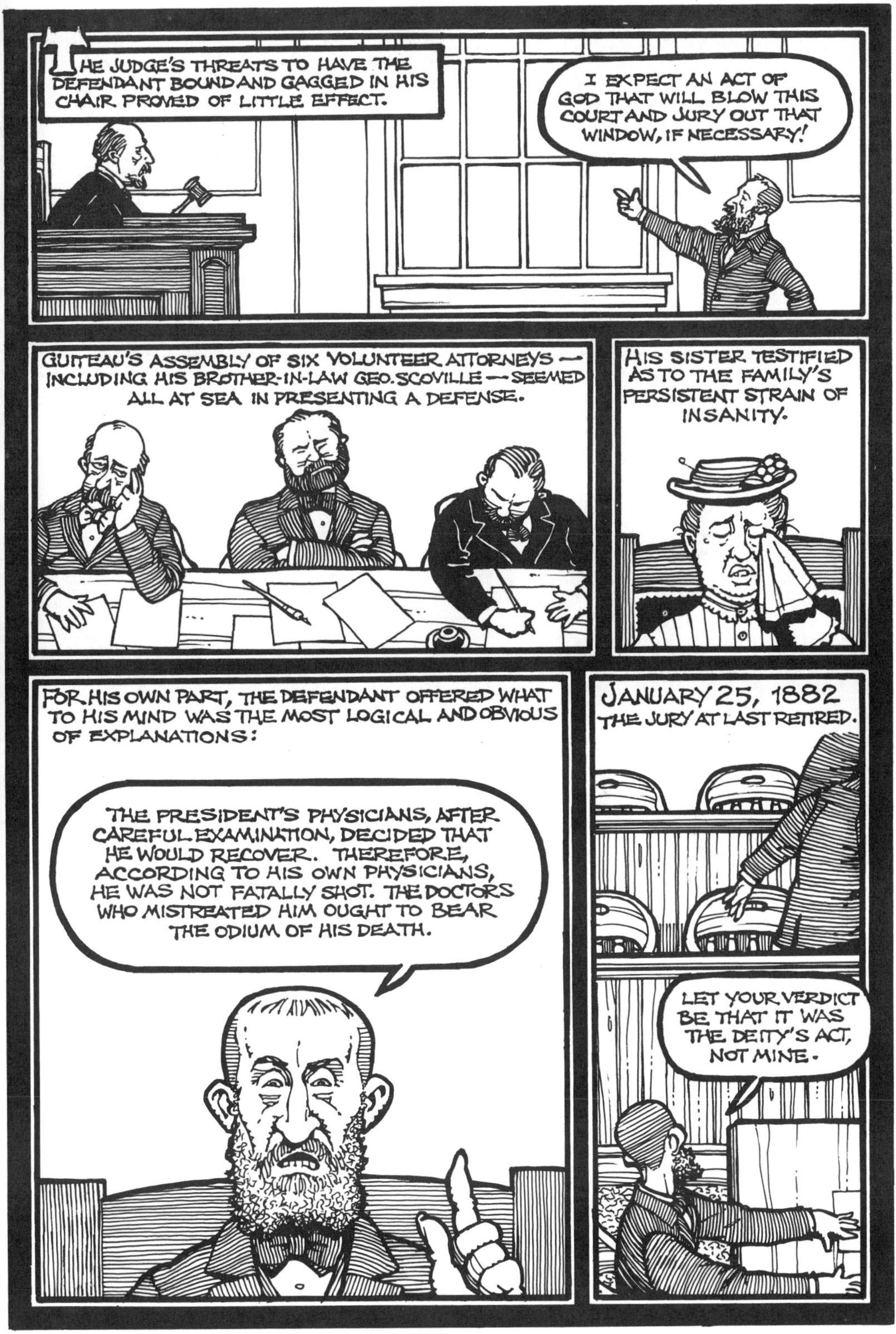
THE JUDGE'S THREATS TO HAVE THE DEFENDANT BOUND AND GAGGED IN HIS CHAIR PROVED OF LITTLE EFFECT.
I EXPECT AN ACT OF GOD THAT WILL BLOW THIS COURT AND JURY OUT THAT WINDOW, IF NECESSARY!
GUITEAU'S ASSEMBLY OF SIX VOLUNTEER ATTORNEYS — INCLUDING HIS BROTHER-IN-LAW GEO. SCOVILLE — SEEMED ALL AT SEA IN PRESENTING A DEFENSE.
HIS SISTER TESTIFIED AS TO THE FAMILY'S PERSISTENT STRAIN OF INSANITY.
FOR HIS OWN PART, THE DEFENDANT OFFERED WHAT TO HIS MIND WAS THE MOST LOGICAL AND OBVIOUS OF EXPLANATIONS:
THE PRESIDENT'S PHYSICIANS, AFTER CAREFUL EXAMINATION, DECIDED THAT HE WOULD RECOVER. THEREFORE, ACCORDING TO HIS OWN PHYSICIANS, HE WAS NOT FATALLY SHOT. THE DOCTORS WHO MISTREATED HIM OUGHT TO BEAR THE ODIUM OF HIS DEATH.
JANUARY 25, 1882
THE JURY AT LAST RETIRED.
LET YOUR VERDICT BE THAT IT WAS THE DEITY'S ACT, NOT MINE.

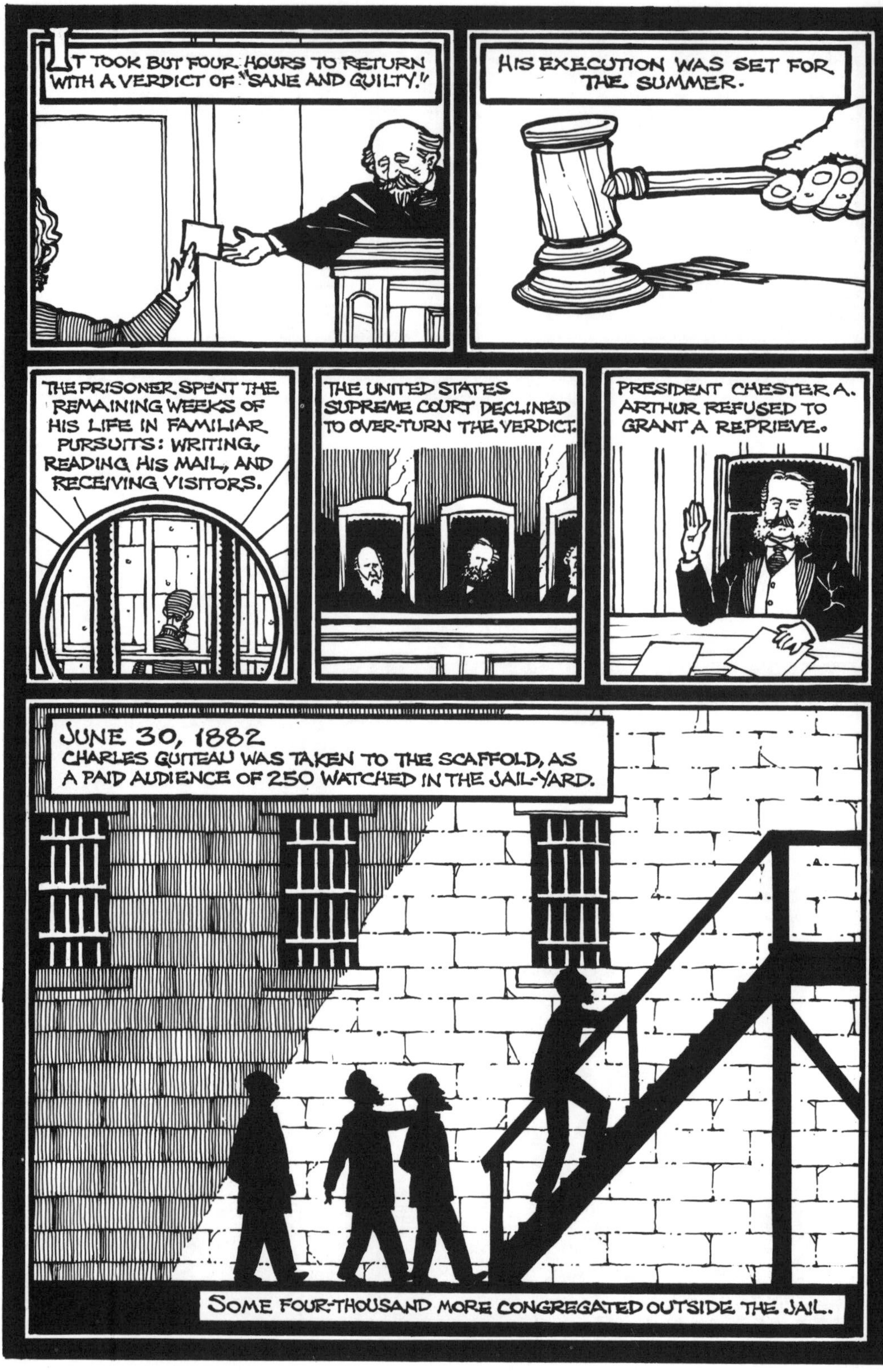
It took but four hours to return with a verdict of "sane and guilty."
His execution was set for the summer.
The prisoner spent the remaining weeks of his life in familiar pursuits: writing, reading his mail, and receiving visitors.
The United States Supreme Court declined to over-turn the verdict.
President Chester A. Arthur refused to grant a reprieve.
June 30, 1882
Charles Guiteau was taken to the scaffold, as a paid audience of 250 watched in the jail-yard.
Some four-thousand more congregated outside the jail.

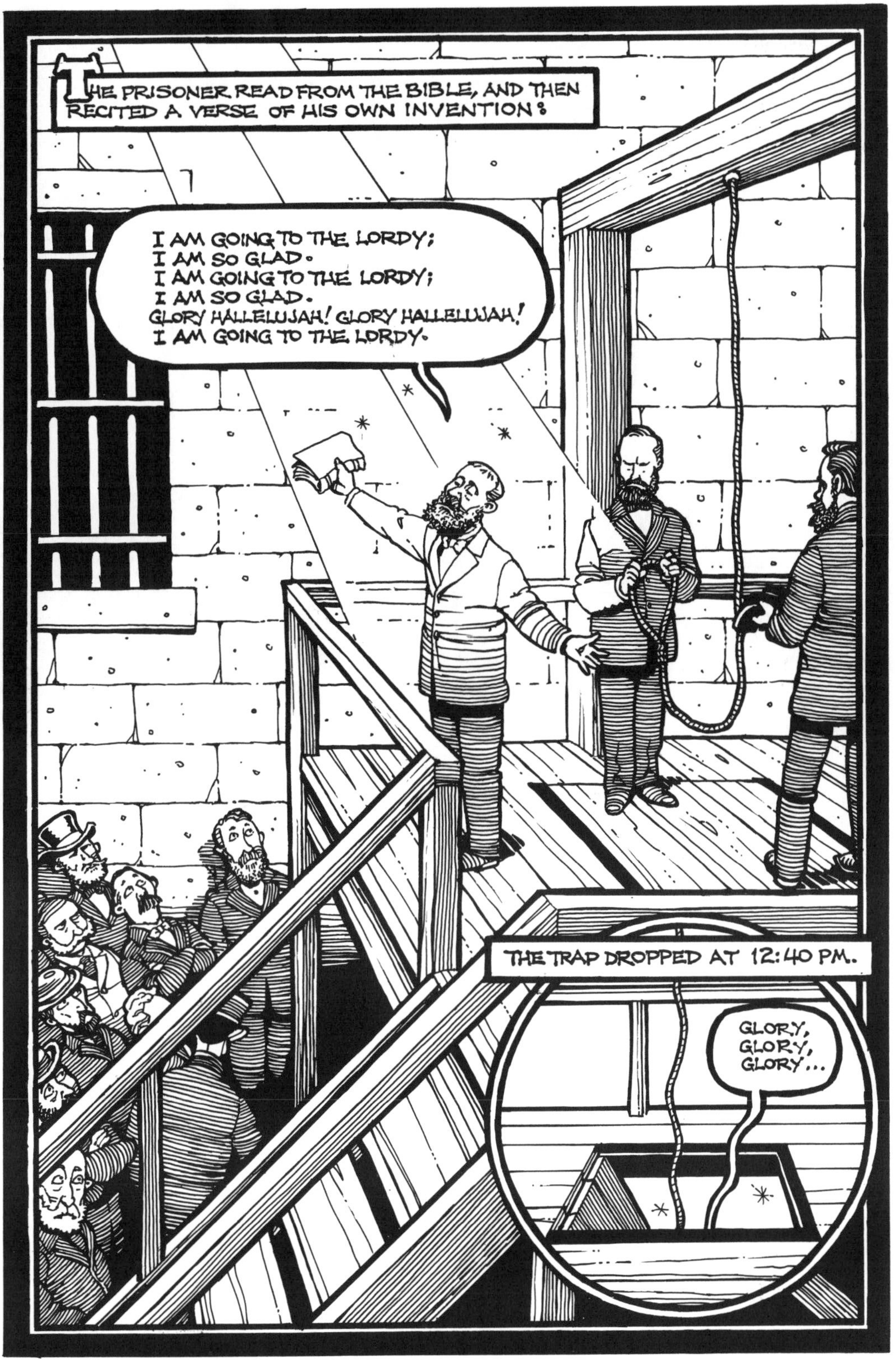
THE PRISONER READ FROM THE BIBLE, AND THEN RECITED A VERSE OF HIS OWN INVENTION:
I AM GOING TO THE LORDY; I AM SO GLAD. I AM GOING TO THE LORDY; I AM SO GLAD. GLORY HALLELUJAH! GLORY HALLELUJAH! I AM GOING TO THE LORDY.
THE TRAP DROPPED AT 12:40 PM.
GLORY, GLORY, GLORY...

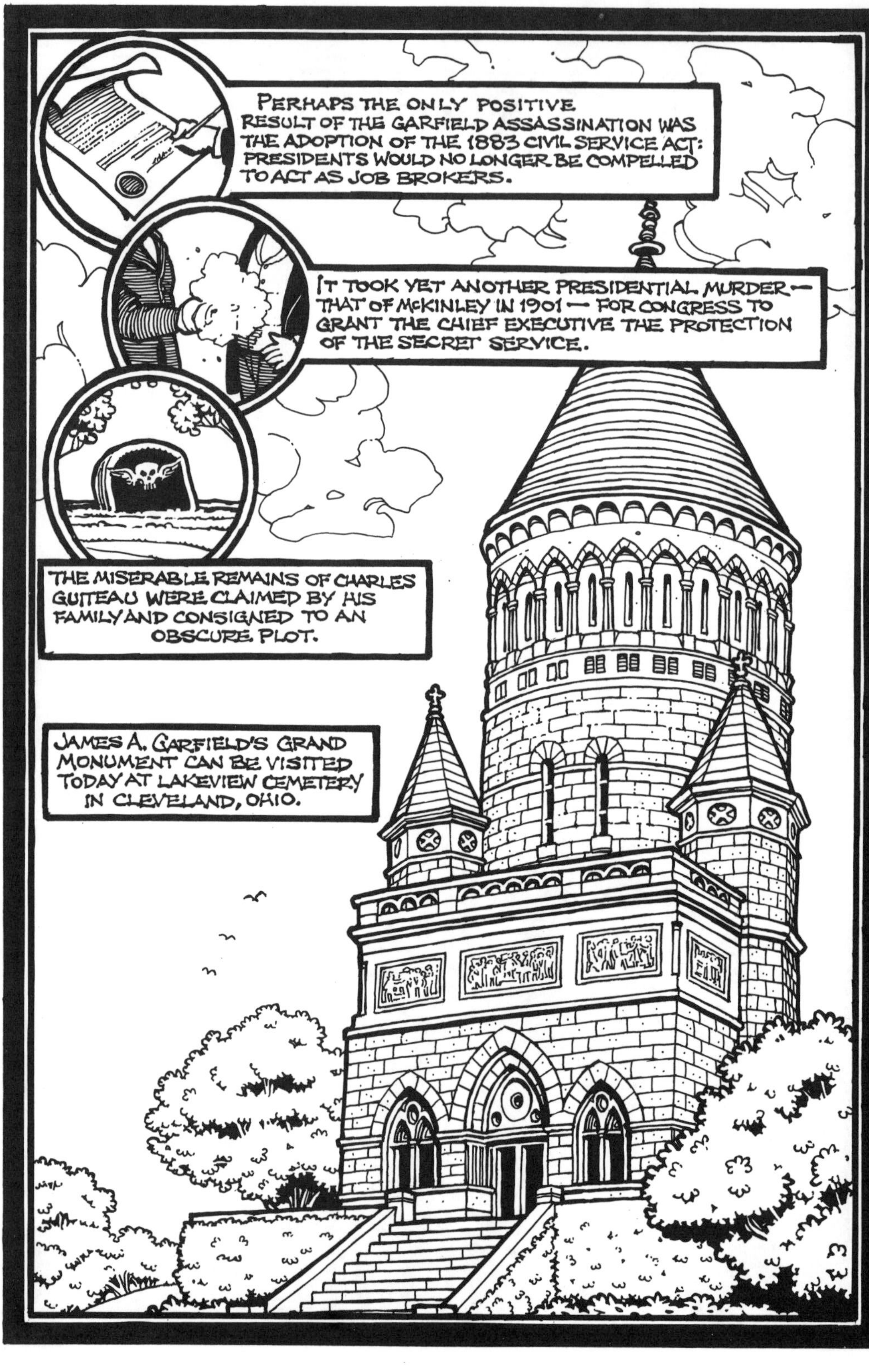
PERHAPS THE ONLY POSITIVE RESULT OF THE GARFIELD ASSASSINATION WAS THE ADOPTION OF THE 1883 CIVIL SERVICE ACT: PRESIDENTS WOULD NO LONGER BE COMPELLED TO ACT AS JOB BROKERS.
IT TOOK YET ANOTHER PRESIDENTIAL MURDER— THAT OF McKINLEY IN 1901 — FOR CONGRESS TO GRANT THE CHIEF EXECUTIVE THE PROTECTION OF THE SECRET SERVICE.
THE MISERABLE REMAINS OF CHARLES GUITEAU WERE CLAIMED BY HIS FAMILY AND CONSIGNED TO AN OBSCURE PLOT.
JAMES A. GARFIELD'S GRAND MONUMENT CAN BE VISITED TODAY AT LAKEVIEW CEMETERY IN CLEVELAND, OHIO.